T0040071

IRRELIGION

ALSO BY JOHN ALLEN PAULOS

Mathematics and Humor: A Study of the Logic of Humor (1980)

I Think, Therefore I Laugh: The Flip Side of Philosophy (1985)

Innumeracy: Mathematical Illiteracy and Its Consequences (1989)

Beyond Numeracy: Ruminations of a Numbers Man (1991)

A Mathematician Reads the Newspaper (1995)

Once Upon a Number: The Hidden Mathematical Logic of Stories (1998)

A Mathematician Plays the Stock Market (2003)

IRRELIGION

*A Mathematician Explains
Why the Arguments for
God Just Don't Add Up*

JOHN ALLEN PAULOS

HILL AND WANG
A division of Farrar, Straus and Giroux
New York

Hill and Wang
A division of Farrar, Straus and Giroux
18 West 18th Street, New York 10011

Printed in the United States of America
Published in 2008 by Hill and Wang
First paperback edition, 2009

The Library of Congress has cataloged the hardcover edition as follows:
Paulos, John Allen.
    Irreligion : a mathematician explains why the arguments for God
just don't add up / by John Allen Paulos. — 1st ed.

        p.   cm.
    Includes index.
    ISBN: 978-0-8090-5919-5 (hardcover : alk. paper)
    1. Irreligion.   2. Atheism.   3. God.   I. Title.

    BL2775.3.P38 2008
    212'.1—dc22

                                                    2007012210

Paperback ISBN: 978-0-8090-5918-8

Designed by Debbie Glasserman

www.fsgbooks.com

P1

*A tip of the hat to my longtime agent, Rafe Sagalyn; my new
editor, Joe Wisnovsky; and all those who've taught me, at times
unintentionally, something about the matters herein.*

For Sheila, Leah, and Daniel, in whom I believe

CONTENTS

Are there any logical reasons to believe in God? Billions of people over thousands of years have entertained this question, and the issue is certainly not without relevance in our world today. The chasms separating literal believers, temperate believers, and outright nonbelievers are deep. There are many who seem to be impressed with the argument that God exists simply because He says He does in a much extolled tome that He allegedly inspired. Many others subscribe with varying degrees of conviction to more sophisticated arguments for God, while atheists and agnostics find none of the arguments persuasive.

Such questions of existence and belief, if not the formal arguments themselves, have always intrigued me. I remember as a child humoring my parents when they discussed Santa Claus with me. I wanted to protect them from my knowledge of his nonexistence, and so I feigned belief. My brother, three years my junior, was only a baby, so it wasn't him I was trying not to disillusion. My qualitative calculations had proved to me that there were too many expectant kids around the world for Mr. Claus to even come close to making his Christmas Eve rounds in time, even if he didn't stop for the occasional hot chocolate. This may sound like quite a pat memory for the author of a book titled *Innumeracy* to have, but I do remember making rough "order of magnitude" calculations that showed that Santa Claus was way overextended.

As I've written elsewhere, if there is an inborn disposition to materialism (in the sense of "matter and motion are the basis of all there is," not in the sense of "I want more cars and houses"), then I suspect I have it. At the risk of being a bit cloying, I remember another early indicator of my adult psychology. I was scuffling with my brother when I was about ten and had an epiphany that the stuff of our two heads wasn't different in kind from the stuff of the rough rug on which I'd just burned my elbow or the stuff of the chair on which he'd just banged his shoulder. The realization that everything was ultimately made out of the same matter, that there was no essential difference between the material compositions of me and not-me, was clean, clear, and bracing.

My youthful materialism quickly evolved into adolescent skepticism, dismissive of just-so tales devoid of evidence. The absence of an answer to the question "What caused, preceded, or created God?" made, in my eyes, the existence of the latter being an unnecessary, antecedent mystery. Why introduce Him? Why postulate a completely nonexplanatory, extra perplexity to help explain the already sufficiently perplexing and beautiful world? Or, if one was committed to such an unnecessary mystery, why not introduce even more antecedent ones such as the Creator's Creator, or even His Great-Uncle?

This vaguely quantitative and logical mind-set no doubt predisposed me to choose the career I have—I'm a mathematician who's morphed into a writer—and to view the world in the way I do. It is what has animated me to write the books and columns I've written, some of which have touched on what I call irreligion—topics, arguments, and questions that spring from an incredulity not only about religion but also about others' credulity. As this and the above anecdotes suggest, I've always found the various arguments for the existence of God that I've come across wanting. There is an inherent illogic to all of the arguments that I've never dealt with head-on. Here in *Irreligion* I've attempted to do so.

My approach in this book is informal and brisk (at least I hope it is), not ceremonious and plodding (at least I hope it isn't). Interspersed among the arguments will be numerous asides on a variety of irreligious themes, ranging from the nature of miracles and creationist probability to cognitive illusions and prudential wagers. Beginning with a schematic outline of an argument, most chapters will briefly examine it and then present what I believe is a succinct deconstruction. The arguments considered range from what might be called the golden oldies of religious thought to those with a more contemporary beat. On the playlist are the first-cause argument, the argument from design, the ontological argument, arguments from faith and biblical codes, the argument from the anthropic principle, the moral universality argument, and others. These arguments overlap to an extent, but I've loosely categorized them in an order that seems somewhat natural.

Don't worry if your mathematical skills are rusty or even completely absent. Although I'm a mathematician, I've not included a single formula in the book. This doesn't mean that mathematics plays little role in what follows. The subject enters in two ways. First, I invoke bits of logic and probability throughout the book, always taking pains in my expositions of them to avoid not only formulas but equations, complicated computations, and technical jargon. Second and more significant, mathematics, or at least my mathematical sensibility, reveals itself in the analytic approach, my choice of examples, and the distaste for extraneous details apparent herein. (Mathematicians are a bit like the laconic Vermonter who, when asked if he's lived in the state his whole life, replies, "Not yet.")

Fully discussing the arguments for God and their refutations, together with the volumes and volumes of commentary and meta-commentary that they continue to generate, brings to mind the predicament of Tristram Shandy. He was the fictional fellow who took two years to write the history of the first two days of his life. In an effort to avoid Shandy's fate and not lose the withered forest for the debunked trees, I've tried in this book—actually more of a handbook or a compendium—to sketch with a lightly heretical touch only the most trenchant refutations of the arguments for God. That is, just the gist, with an occasional jest. These refutations—some new and idiosyncratic, but many dating back centuries or even millennia—are not nearly as widely known as they once were, and therefore, I believe, there is value in having them all available in one place. (For this reason I've here adapted some sections from the other books and columns of mine that I mentioned above.)

This effort is especially important now given this country's rampant scripture-spouting religiosity and the policies and debacles to which it has already led and to which it may further lead. A representative of the Enlightenment, which, unfortunately, sometimes seems to be in the process of being repealed, Voltaire presciently observed, "Those who can make you believe absurdities can make you commit atrocities." This dire forecast is all the more likely to come to pass when politicians and a substantial portion of a large political party are among the most effective purveyors of beliefs such as the "Rapture." (On the other hand, I have little problem with those who acknowledge the absence of good arguments for God, but simply maintain a nebulous but steadfast belief in "something more.")

The first step in untangling religious absurdities is to recognize that the arguments for the existence of God depend on the definition of God. Who or what is God? Some authors write that He is ineffable or define Him in some idiosyncratic manner as synonymous with nature or with the laws of physics or in an indeterminate number of other ways.

Most conventional monotheistic characterizations of God (Yahweh, Allah), however, take Him to be an entity or being that is, if not omnipotent, at least extraordinarily powerful; if not omniscient, at least surpassingly wise; if not the Creator of the universe, at least intimately connected with its origin; if not completely and absolutely perfect, at least possessor of all manner of positive characteristics. This formulation will, on the whole, be my definition of God, and the many flawed arguments for this entity's existence will be my primary focus. Different traditions adorn Him with different narratives and attributes, but I'll discuss neither these nor the broader cultures and attitudes associated with specific religions.

An atheist I'll take to be someone who believes that such an entity does not exist, and an agnostic I'll take to be someone who believes that whether God exists or not is either unknown, unknowable, or a meaningless question. (I won't discuss complex intermediate cases, represented in my mind by a friend who professes to being an atheist but, when asked why he adheres strictly to religious rituals, replies, "Because God commands it.") Contrary to some, I think it's certainly possible to be both an atheist and an agnostic. Think, for example, of the innumerable historical figures or events in whose existence or occurrence we don't believe, but about whose existence and occurrence we're not absolutely sure. The definitions of these terms are, of course, sensitive to the definition of God to which one subscribes. Define God in a sufficiently nebulous way as beauty, love, mysterious complexity, or the ethereal taste of strawberry shortcake, and most atheists become theists. Still, although one can pose as Humpty Dumpty and aver, "When I use a word, it means just what I choose it to mean, neither more nor less," others needn't play along.

One question people interested in the matters discussed in this book often have is whether, despite my present views, I ever had or perhaps somehow still have a formal religion. There is, of course, a significant difference between the formal religion one is born into or with which one is otherwise associated and one's true beliefs. There are many paths to an irreligious outlook, my own, as I've indicated above, being somewhat straightforward. I simply never had a religious phase. As a consequence, I am not now renouncing a faith I once had, and this book isn't intended as a sort of Epistle of Paulos the Apostate to the Theologians. Although raised in a nominally Christian home (my grandparents emigrated from Greece) and ensconced now in a secular Jewish family, I never found either religion's doctrines intellectually or emotionally palatable, much less compelling.

This is not to say that I don't value at least parts of some religious traditions, ideals, and festivals (ranging from Passover to Thailand's Loy Krathong). Nor is it to say I don't acknowledge that there have been untold people who have selflessly served others in the name of their God. Nor is it to say that I don't recognize that many intelligent people are religious. I mean merely to say that I am and always have been an atheist/agnostic and will herein attempt to explain why perhaps you should be, too.

Let me end these preliminaries by noting that although a nonbeliever, I've always wondered about the possibility of a basic proto-religion acceptable to atheists and agnostics. By this I mean a "religion" that has no dogma, no narratives, and no existence claims and yet still acknowledges the essential awe and wonder of the world and perhaps affords as well an iota of serenity. The best I've been able to come up with is the "Yeah-ist" religion, whose response to the intricacy, beauty, and mystery of the world is a simple affirmation and acceptance, "Yeah," and whose only prayer is the one word "Yeah." This minimalist "Yeah-ist" religion is consistent with more complex religions (but not with the "Nah" religion) and with an irreligious ethics and a liberating, self-mediated stance toward life and its stories. Furthermore, it conforms nicely with a scientific perspective and with the idea that the certainty of uncertainty is the only kind of certainty we can expect.

So, Yeah, let's move on to the arguments for God's existence.

FOUR
CLASSICAL
ARGUMENTS

The Argument from First Cause
(and Unnecessary Intermediaries)

The very first phrase of the Book of Genesis, "In the beginning," suggests the first-cause argument for the existence of God. In clarifying the argument's structure, Bertrand Russell cites a seemingly different account of the beginning—the Hindu myth that the world rests on an elephant and the elephant rests on a tortoise. When asked about the tortoise, the Hindu replies, "Suppose we change the subject."

But let's not change the subject. As I will throughout the book, I begin with a rough schema of the argument in question:

1. Everything has a cause, or perhaps many causes.
2. Nothing is its own cause.
3. Causal chains can't go on forever.

4. So there has to be a first cause.

5. That first cause is God, who therefore exists.

If we assume the everyday understanding of the word "cause" and accept the above argument, then it's natural to identify God with the first cause. God's the one, according to a religious acquaintance of mine, who "got the ball rolling." A slight variation of this is the so-called cosmological argument, which dates back to Aristotle and depends on the Big Bang theory of the origins of the universe (or some primitive precursor to it). It states that whatever has a beginning must have a cause and since the universe is thought to have a beginning, it must have a cause.

So have we found God? Is He simply the Prime Bowler or the Big Banger? Does this clinch it? Of course not. The argument doesn't even come close. One gaping hole in it is Assumption 1, which might be better formulated as: Either everything has a cause or there's something that doesn't. The first-cause argument collapses into this hole whichever tack we take. If everything has a cause, then God does, too, and there is no first cause. And if something doesn't have a cause, it may as well be the physical world as God or a tortoise.

Of someone who asserts that God is the uncaused first cause (and then preens as if he's really explained something), we should thus inquire, "Why cannot the physical world itself be taken to be the uncaused first cause?" After all, the venerable principle of Occam's razor advises us to "shave off" unnecessary assumptions, and taking the world itself as the uncaused first cause has the great virtue of not introducing the unnecessary hypothesis of God.

Moreover, all the questions stimulated by accepting the uncaused existence of the physical world—Why is it here? How did it come about? and, of course, What caused it?—can as easily and appropriately be asked of God. Why is God here? How did He come about? What caused Him? (This reflexive tack is not unrelated to the childhood taunt of "What about your mama?" Rather, it's "What about your papa?") The cogency of this sort of response to the first-cause argument is indicated by Saint Augustine's exasperated reaction to a version of it. When he was asked what God was doing before He made the world, Augustine supposedly answered, "He was creating a hell for people who ask questions like that."

A related objection to the argument is that the uncaused first cause needn't have any traditional God-like qualities. It's simply first, and as we know from other realms, being first doesn't mean being best. No one brags about still using the first personal computers to come on the market. Even if the first cause existed, it might simply be a brute fact—or even worse, an actual brute.

Furthermore, efforts by some to put God, the putative first cause, completely outside of time and space give up entirely on the notion of cause, which is defined in terms of time. After all, *A* causes *B* only if *A* comes before *B*, and the first cause comes—surprise—first, before its consequences. (Placing God outside of space and time would also preclude any sort of later divine intervention in worldly affairs.) In fact, ordinary language breaks down when we contemplate these matters. The phrase "beginning of time," for example, can't rely on the same presuppositions that "beginning of the movie" can. Before a movie there's popcorn-buying and coming attractions; there isn't any popcorn-buying, coming attractions, or anything else before the universe.

The notion of cause has still other problems. It is nowhere near as clear and robust as it was before the eighteenth-century Scottish philosopher David Hume and twentieth-century quantum mechanics finished qualifying it. Hume argued that the phrase "A causes B" means nothing more than "A has been followed by B in every instance we've examined." Every time we've dropped the rock, it's fallen. Since it's quite easy to imagine our dropping of the rock not being followed by its falling, however, the connection between cause and effect cannot be a logically necessary connection. The link between an event and its causes is contingent and rather squishy. We can't move as confidently from an event to its cause(s) as we might have believed. Causes are discoverable by experience, but not by armchair a priori reasoning, making "cause" much less sturdy a notion than the first-cause argument presupposes. Constructing a structure out of steel is much easier than building one out of noodles, and arguments are metaphorically somewhat similar.

And if to Hume's and other modern accounts of causality and scientific induction we add the implication of quantum mechanics that "cause" at the micro level is at best probabilistic (not to mention all the quantum weirdnesses that have been cataloged by physicists), the first-cause argument loses much of its limited force. In fact, some versions of quantum cosmology explicitly rule out a first cause. Other accounts imply that the Big Bang and the birth of universes are recurring phenomena.

Interestingly, the so-called natural-law argument for the existence of God has a structure similar to the first-cause argument and is thus vulnerable to a similar bit of jujitsu. It can even be explained to the chattering little offspring in the backseat. He is the one who asks, "Why is that, Daddy?" and responds to your explanation with another "Why?" He then responds to your more general explanation with "Why?" once again, and on and on. Eventually you answer, "Because that's the way it is." If this satisfies the kid, the game is over, but if it goes on for another round and you're a religious sort, you might respond with "Because God made it that way." If this satisfies, the game is over, but what if the kid still persists?

Phrased a bit more formally, the natural-law argument points to the physical regularities that have been laboriously discovered by physicists and other natural scientists and posits God as the lawgiver, the author of these laws. Whatever power the argument has, however, is greatly diminished by asking, as the endearingly curious kid might, why God "made it that way." That is, why did He create the particular natural laws that He did? If He did it arbitrarily for no reason at all, there is then something that is not subject to natural law. The chain of natural law is broken, and so we might as well take the most general natural laws themselves, rather than God, as the arbitrary final "Because." On the other hand, if He had a reason for issuing the particular laws that He did (say, to bring about the best possible universe), then God Himself is subject to preexisting constraints, standards, and laws. In this case, too, there's not much point to introducing Him as an intermediary in the first place.

Still, philosophers ranging from Aristotle to Aquinas to Gottfried Leibniz have insisted that something must explain the universe—its laws and even its very existence. Leibniz famously and succinctly asked, "Why is there something rather than nothing?" Indeed, why is there stuff? Invoking his principle of sufficient reason, which states that there must be sufficient reason (or cause) for every fact, he answered his own question. The sufficient reason for the universe, he stated, "is a necessary Being bearing the reason for its existence within itself." The necessary being is God, the first cause, who caused or brought about not only the physical world but also somehow Himself.

This suggests that one reasonable reaction to these refutations of the first-cause and natural-law arguments is to question Assumption 2 that nothing is its own cause. Some have tried to make logical sense of the first cause causing not only the second cause(s) but also itself or, analogously, the most general law explaining not only the next most general law(s) but also itself. The late philosopher Robert Nozick considers such self-subsumptive principles in his book *Philosophical Explanations*. There he entertains the idea of an abstract self-subsumptive principle, P, of the following type: P says that any law-like statement having characteristic C is true. Principle P is used to explain why other, less general laws hold true. They hold true because they have characteristic C. And what would explain why P holds true? A possible answer might be that P itself also has characteristic C. In short, P, if true, would explain itself.

Even Nozick acknowledged that this "appears quite weird—a feat of legerdemain." Still, there are not many alternatives. The chain of causes (laws) is either finite or infinite. If it's finite, the most basic cause (most general law) is either a brute, arbitrary fact or self-subsuming. Nozick also wrote of certain yogic mystical exercises that help to bring about the experiential analogue of self-subsumption. He theorized that "one of the acts the (male) yogis perform, during their experiences of being identical with infinitude, is auto-fellatio, wherein they have an intense and ecstatic experience of self-generation, of the universe and themselves turned back upon itself in a self-creation." This isn't the traditional image of the Creator, and, if so moved, the reader may supply his own joke here.

The Argument from Design
(and Some Creationist Calculations)

The trees swaying in the breeze, the gentle hills and valleys, the lakes teeming with fish, are all beautifully exquisite. How could there not be a God? One of the most familiar sentiments behind arguments for the existence of God, this one points to the complexity and/or purpose inherent in nature. So-called teleological arguments (or arguments from design) vary slightly in form, but all attribute this perceived purpose or complexity to a divine creator. This is their basic structure:

1. Something—the diversity of life-forms, the beauty of the outdoors, the stars, the fine structure constants—is much too complex (or too perfect) to have come about randomly or by sheer accident.

2. This something must have been the handiwork of some creator.
3. Therefore God, the Creator, exists.

An alternative version points to the purpose that some see permeating nature:

1. The world in general or life-forms in it seem to be evidence of clear intention or direction.
2. There must be an intender or director behind this purpose.
3. This entity must be God, and therefore God exists.

I should first mention that there are unobjectionable uses of teleological explanations, ones that make reference to purpose and intention, especially when such explanations can be easily reformulated in nonpurposive terms. For example, "The thermostat is trying to keep the house at a steady temperature" can be rephrased in terms of metals' differential rates of expansion. When it gets hot, this metal expands faster than the other one and tips a switch turning the furnace off, and when it gets cool, the metal contracts faster, turning the furnace back on. No one is really attributing intentionality to the metals.

The teleological argument dates back to the Greeks, but probably its best-known proponent is the English theologian William Paley, whose watchmaker analogy is often cited by creation scientists and others. Paley asks us to imagine wandering around an uncultivated field and coming upon a watch lying on the ground. He compares evidence of design in the watch, which all would certainly acknowledge, to the evidence of design in nature—plants, animals, and the like. Just as the watch clearly had a human creator, Paley argues, the designs in nature must have had a divine creator. (Exclaiming "Oh my God!" upon discovering a gold Rolex next to some beautiful flowers does not count in the argument's favor.)

Interestingly, this watch analogy goes back even further, to Cicero, whose clocks, however, were sundials and water clocks. Watches with simple quartz and silicon components and their future refinements might also be cited. Although all these timekeeping devices could be taken to be something else (the latter might be confused, for example, with sand on a beach), people are familiar with their own cultural artifacts and would still recognize their human provenance. We know what humans make, but no such familiarity can be assumed with the alleged divine artifacts.

The most glaring weakness in teleological arguments is, however, Assumption 1. What is the probability of such complexity? How do we know that something is too complex to have arisen by itself? What is the origin of this complexity? Creationists explain what they regard as the absurdly unlikely complexity of life-forms by postulating a creator. That this creator would have to be of vastly greater complexity and vastly more unlikely than the life-forms it created does not seem to bother them. Nonetheless, it's only natural to ask the same question of the creator as one does of the alleged creations. Laying down a recursive card similar to that played with the first-cause argument, we ask about the origin of the creator's complexity. How did it come about? Is there a whole hierarchy of creators, each created by higher-order creators and all except for the lowliest, ours, creating lower-order ones?

Let me underline this last irreligious bit in a slightly different manner. If a certain entity is very complex and it's deemed extraordinarily unlikely that such complexity would have arisen by itself, then what is explained by attributing the entity's unlikely complexity to an even more complex and even more unlikely source? This creationist Ponzi scheme quickly leads to metaphysical bankruptcy.

I remember the girlfriend of a college roommate who had apparently misunderstood something she'd read on mnemonic devices. To memorize a telephone number, for example, she might have recalled that her best friend had two children, her dentist had five, her camp roommate three, her neighbor on one side had three dogs, the one on the other side seven cats, her older brother had eight children if you counted those of his wives, and she herself was one of four children. The telephone number must be 253-3784. Her mnemonics were convoluted, inventive, amusing, unrelated to any other structure, and always very much longer than what they were designed to help her remember. They also seem to make the same mistake creationists make when they "explain" complexity by invoking a greater complexity.

The beguiling metaphor that the argument from design appeals to can also be phrased in terms of a large Lego model of, say, Notre Dame Cathedral. If one came upon it, one would be compelled to say that the blocks were put together by intelligent humans. Furthermore, if the model was taken apart and placed in a large bag and the bag was shaken for a long time, one would be quite resistant to the idea that the Lego pieces would fashion themselves into a cathedral again.

Of course, the real problem with Assumption 1 is that, unlike the situation with the Lego model, there is a well-confirmed alternative explanation for the origin of life's complexity (and wondrous unity and diversity), and—trumpets here—that is Darwin's theory of evolution. But creation science and its purportedly more scientific descendant, the theory of intelligent design, reject evolution as being unable to explain the complexity of life. Creationists insist that DNA's basic amino acid building blocks are like the Lego pieces and couldn't have put themselves together "by accident." Doing so, they argue, would be too improbable.

I should note in passing that they also sometimes cite the second law of thermodynamics as providing evidence for their position. The second law states that in a closed system, entropy (or, roughly but a bit misleadingly, disorder) always increases. The glass pitcher breaks, coffee disperses in milk, air escapes from a punctured balloon, and these things don't happen in reverse. Creationists sometimes point to humans, plants, and animals as being counterexamples to the second law since they often become more ordered with time. There is a very detailed response to this, but here is a very short one: since living things are open to their surroundings and the earth is open to the sun, they are clearly not closed systems and hence not counterexamples to the second law. Local human decreases in entropy are perfectly consistent with thermodynamics.

The results of a recent international study in the journal *Science* by Professor Jon Miller of Michigan State University and his associates document the prevalence of beliefs of the above sort about the origins of life. Their study finds not only that a growing number of Americans do not believe in the theory of evolution but that of thirty-two European nations and Japan, only Turkey has a higher percentage of its citizens rejecting Darwin. The authors attribute the results in the United States to religious fundamentalism, inadequate science education, and partisan political maneuvering. With regard to the latter Miller notes, "There is no major political party in Europe and Japan that uses opposition to evolution as a part of its political platform."

There's another contributing factor to this opposition to evolution that I want to briefly discuss here. It is the concerted attempt by creationists to dress up in the garb of mathematics fundamentalist claims about human origins and to focus criticism on what they take to be the minuscule probability of evolutionary development. (Even the conservative television pundit and ace biologist Ann Coulter has lent her perspicacity to this mathematical endeavor in her recent book *Godless: The Church of Liberalism*.)

Creationists argue that the likelihood that, say, a new species of horse will develop is absurdly tiny. The same, they say, is true of the development of the eye or some physiological system or mechanism.

A bit more precisely the argument goes roughly as follows: A very long sequence of individually improbable mutations must occur in order for a species or a biological process to evolve. If we assume these are independent events, then the probability that all of them will occur and that they will occur in the right order is the product of their respective probabilities, which is always a tiny number. Thus, for example, the probability of getting a 3, 2, 6, 2, and 5 when rolling a single die five times is $\frac{1}{6} \times \frac{1}{6} \times \frac{1}{6} \times \frac{1}{6} \times \frac{1}{6}$, or $\frac{1}{7,776}$—one chance in 7,776. The much longer sequences of fortuitous events necessary for a new species or a new process to evolve lead to the minuscule probabilities that creationists argue prove that evolution is so wildly improbable as to be essentially impossible.

This line of argument, however, is deeply flawed. Note that there are always a fantastically huge number of evolutionary paths that might be taken by an organism (or a process), but there is only one that will actually be taken. So if, after the fact, we observe the particular evolutionary path actually taken and then calculate the a priori probability of its having been taken, we will get the minuscule probability that creationists mistakenly attach to the process as a whole.

Leaving aside the issues of independence, fitness landscapes, and randomness (all analogies are limited), I offer another example. We have a deck of cards before us. There are almost 10^{68}—a 1 with 68 zeros after it—orderings of the fifty-two cards in the deck. Any of the fifty-two cards might be first, any of the remaining fifty-one second, any of the remaining fifty third, and so on. This is a humongous number, but it's not hard to devise even everyday situations that give rise to much larger numbers. Now, if we shuffle this deck of cards for a long time and then examine the particular ordering of the cards that happens to result, we would be justified in concluding that the probability of this particular ordering of the cards having occurred is approximately one chance in 10^{68}. This probability certainly qualifies as minuscule.

Still, we would not be justified in concluding that the shuffles could not have possibly resulted in this particular ordering because its a priori probability is so very tiny. Some ordering had to result from the shuffling, and this one did. Nor, of course, would we be justified in concluding that the whole process of moving from one ordering to another via shuffles is so wildly improbable as to be practically impossible.

The actual result of the shufflings will always have a minuscule probability of occurring, but, unless you're a creationist, that doesn't mean the process of obtaining the result is at all dubious. The *Science* study is disturbing for many reasons, not the least of which is that there's no telling to what length the creationist trunk of the GOP elephant will evolve.

A related creationist argument is supplied by Michael Behe, a key supporter of intelligent design. Behe likens what he terms the "irreducible complexity" of phenomena such as the clotting of blood to the irreducible complexity of a mousetrap. If just one of the trap's pieces is missing—whether it be the spring, the metal platform, or the board—the trap is useless. The implicit suggestion is that all the parts of a mousetrap would have had to come into being at once, an impossibility unless there were an intelligent designer. Design proponents argue that what's true for the mousetrap is all the more true for vastly more complex biological phenomena. If any of the twenty or so proteins involved in blood-clotting is absent, for example, clotting doesn't occur, and so, the creationist argument goes, these proteins must have all been brought into being at once by a designer.

But the theory of evolution does explain the evolution of complex biological organisms and phenomena, and the Paley argument from design has been decisively refuted. For the record, natural selection is a highly nonrandom process that acts on the genetic variation produced by random mutation and genetic drift and results in those organisms with more adaptive traits differentially surviving and reproducing. It's not a case of monkeys simply randomly pecking Shakespeare on a conventional typewriter. It's more akin to monkeys randomly pecking on a special typewriter that marginally more often than not retains correct letters and deletes incorrect ones. (Oddly, the fact that we and all life have evolved from simpler forms by natural selection disturbs fundamentalists who are completely unfazed by the biblical claim that we come from dirt.)

Further rehashing of defenses of Darwin or refutations of Paley is not my goal, however. Those who reject evolution are usually immune to such arguments anyway. Rather, my intention finally is to develop some telling analogies between these biological issues and related economic ones and, secondarily, to show that these analogies point to a surprising crossing of political lines.

How is it that modern free-market economies are as complex as they are, boasting amazingly elaborate production, distribution, and communication systems? Go into almost any drugstore and you can find your favorite candy bar. Every supermarket has your brand of spaghetti sauce, or the store down the block does. Your size and style of jeans are in every neighborhood.

And what's true at the personal level is true at the industrial level. Somehow there are enough ball bearings and computer chips in just the right places in factories all over the country. The physical infrastructure and communication networks are also marvels of integrated complexity. Oil and gas supplies are, by and large, where they're needed. Your e-mail reaches you in Miami as well as in Milwaukee, not to mention Barcelona and Bangkok.

The natural question, discussed first by Adam Smith and later by Friedrich Hayek and Karl Popper, among others, is, Who designed this marvel of complexity? Which commissar decreed the number of packets of dental floss for each retail outlet? The answer, of course, is that no economic god designed this system. It emerged and grew by itself, a stunningly obvious example of spontaneously evolving order. No one argues that all the components of the candy bar distribution system must have been put into place at once or else there would be no Snickers at the corner store.

So far, so good. What is more than a bit odd, however, is that some of the most ardent opponents of Darwinian evolution—for example, many fundamentalist Christians—are among the most ardent supporters of the free market. These people accept the natural complexity of the market without qualm, yet they insist that the natural complexity of biological phenomena requires a designer.

They would reject the idea that there is or should be central planning in the economy. They would rightly point out that simple economic exchanges that are beneficial to people become entrenched and then gradually modified and improved as they become part of larger systems of exchange, while those that are not beneficial die out. They accept the claim that Adam Smith's invisible hand brings about the spontaneous order of the modern economy. Yet, as noted, some of these same people refuse to believe that natural selection and "blind processes" can lead to similar biological order arising spontaneously. And their refusals, if responses to some of my irreligiously tinged books and columns are at all typical, generally range from vituperative to venomous with most clustering around the latter.

Nor is great intelligence required. Software dating back to the mathematician John Horton Conway's game of Life utilizes very simple mindless rules of interaction between virtual "agents" and leads to similar sorts of economic complexity. So do genetic algorithms and models involving the cellular automatons of Stephen Wolfram and many others, which I'll touch on later.

These ideas are not new. As mentioned, Smith, Hayek, Popper, and others have made them more or less explicitly. Recently, there have appeared several more mathematical echoes of these analogies invoking network, complexity, and systems theory. These include an essay by Kelley L. Ross as well as briefer comments by Mark Kleiman and Jim Lindgren.

There are, of course, quite significant differences and disanalogies between biological systems and economic ones (one being that biology is a much more substantive science than economics), but these shouldn't blind us to their similarities or mask the obvious analogies.

These analogies prompt two final questions. What would you think of someone who studied economic entities and their interactions in a modern free-market economy and insisted that they were, despite a perfectly reasonable and empirically supported account of their development, the consequence of some all-powerful, detail-obsessed economic lawgiver? You might deem such a person a conspiracy theorist.

And what would you think of someone who studied biological processes and organisms and insisted that they were, despite a perfectly reasonable and empirically supported Darwinian account of their development, the consequence of some all-powerful, detail-obsessed biological lawgiver?

A Personally Crafted Pseudoscience

In anticipation of the arguments from the anthropic principle and coincidence to be presented in later chapters, I want to provide a whimsical mathematical recipe for anyone who might want to develop his or her very own pseudoscience. The Dutch astronomer Cornelis de Jager, who concocted the following algorithm for personalized physical constants, used it to advance a charming theory about the metaphysical properties of Dutch bicycles.

Here's the recipe: Think of any four numbers associated with yourself (your height or weight, the number of children you have, your birthday or anniversary, whatever) and label them X, Y, Z, and W. Now consider various products and powers of these numbers. Specifically consider the expression $X^a \, Y^b \, Z^c \, W^d$, where the exponents a, *b*, *c*, and *d* range over the values 0, 1, 2, 3, 4, 5, $\frac{1}{2}$, $\frac{1}{3}$, $\frac{1}{4}$, or the negatives of these numbers. (For any number *N*, $N^{\frac{1}{2}}$, $N^{\frac{1}{3}}$, and $N^{\frac{1}{4}}$ equal the square root, cube root, and fourth root of *N*, respectively, and *N* to a negative exponent, say N^{-2}, is equal to 1 over *N* to the corresponding positive exponent, $\frac{1}{N^2}$.) Since each of the four exponents may be any one of these 17 numbers, the number of possible choices of *a*, *b*, *c*, and *d* is, by the multiplication principle, 83,521 ($17 \times 17 \times 17 \times 17$). There are thus this many values for the expression $X^a\, Y^b\, Z^c\, W^d$.

Among all these values, there will likely be several that equal, to at least a couple of decimal places, universal constants such as the speed of light, the gravitational constant, Planck's constant, the fine structure constant, the boiling point of carbon, and so on. If there are not, the units in which these constants or your personal numbers are expressed can be altered to get the required equality. A computer program can easily be written that checks to see which of these universal constants is equal to one of the 83,521 numbers generated from your original four numbers.

Thus you might learn that for your particular personal numbers *X*, *Y*, *Z*, and *W* the number $X^2\, Y^{\frac{1}{3}}\, Z^{-3}\, W^{-1}$ is equal to the sun's distance from the earth in miles (or kilometers or inches). Or you might discover any of a host of other correspondences between your personal numbers and these universal constants. The recipe can clearly be revised and developed further, but using some version of it, you get to revel in some marvelous correspondence between your little numbers and the world's cosmic constants.

De Jager, a biking enthusiast, found that the square of his bike's pedal diameter multiplied by the square root of the product of the diameters of his bell and light was equal to 1,836, the ratio of the mass of a proton to that of an electron. Incidentally, the ratio of the height of the Sears Tower in Chicago to the height of the Woolworth Building in New York is the same to four significant digits (1.836 versus 1,836) as the above figure. Just maybe the correspondences generated in this way betoken a personal God. Yeah, right.

Although the above isn't particularly amusing, it isn't reverential, either, and does suggest a couple of questions about religion and humor. Why is the notion of a fundamentalist comedian funny, or at least quite odd? Why does the idea of God as a comedian seem more appealing (at least to me) than the traditional view of God? Why does solemnity tend to infect almost all discussions of religion? Certainly an inability or reluctance to stand outside one's preferred framework is part of the answer. So is an intolerance for tentativeness and whimsy. The incongruity necessary for appreciating humor is only recognizable with an open mind and fresh perspective. (A famous "argument" for an abstract proposition symbolized by p comes to mind. It's ascribed to the philosopher Sidney Morgenbesser and illustrates, or maybe mocks, this fluid capriciousness. "So if not p, what? q maybe?")

Anyway, a minister, a rabbi, an imam, and an angry atheist, each believing in the strict literal truth (or literal falsity) of his holy scriptures, were opening at the Improv and . . .

The Argument from the Anthropic Principle (and a Probabilistic Doomsday)

Everything in the world seems just right for little old us. This is a durable idea, as evidenced by Voltaire's quip "Observe, for instance, the nose is formed for spectacles." Surely something must explain this "just rightness." Updated and more precisely put, the idea becomes the anthropic principle, which states that the basic physical constants of our universe are "fine-tuned" to allow us to exist, and were they not so precisely tuned, we wouldn't be around and able to observe it. This leads to a more scientifically sophisticated version of the argument from design with God as the fine-tuner in charge:

1. The values of physical constants, the matter-antimatter imbalance, and various other physical laws are necessary for human beings to exist.
2. Human beings exist.
3. The physics must have been fine-tuned to the constants' values to make us possible.
4. Therefore the fine-tuner, God, exists.

Clearly the jump from Assumptions 1 and 2 to 3 in the argument sketched above is one of the weakest aspects of this argument. What does follow from Assumptions 1 and 2 above is simply that the values of the constants are what they are. Discussion of the anthropic principle is sensitive to which of its many flavors—ranging from the empty to the unwarranted—is being tasted. Some scientists say that the principle is tautological, a fancy way of saying, "If things—the constants, the stars, life-forms—were different, well, then they'd be different." They note that nothing is explained by intoning that in order for us to exist to observe the universe, its laws and constants must allow for observers such as us to exist.

Another response to the anthropic principle is that other, perhaps non-carbon-based forms of life are possible and would develop were the constants or physical laws different or were the intervals of life-allowing values for the physical constants larger than the principle assumes (as they well might be). In other words, if the constants or laws were different, different life-forms might have developed, possibly even to the point where they would be discussing the fine-tuning that allows them to exist. Still other responses note that physical laws and constants may not be invariant throughout the universe (our region, but not others, allowing life to develop), or that there may be many universes, each with different laws and constants.

The physicist Lee Smolin has even postulated a kind of evolution of universes, whereby new "baby" universes are born when black holes are formed in other "parent" universes. These baby universes have slightly different constants and laws, and Smolin has hypothesized that a universe giving rise to more black holes (and thus differentially flourishing) would have the physical constants and laws that our universe does. Despite what initially seems to be an outlandish theory, this is, as Smolin notes, at least a falsifiable one.

Less fraught with speculative physics and dubious metaphysics than the anthropic principle is the related phenomenon of self-selection, the drawing of inferences from our own existence. One interesting application of self-selection that has a quasi-religious feel to it is the so-called Doomsday argument.

Doomsday, so many ways for it to occur. Is the sky falling? And if so, when? Even when they're sometimes baseless, constant reports about nuclear weapons proliferation, pandemic diseases like bird flu, wars in the Middle

East, and global warming, among other environmental catastrophes, revive these perennial human questions and contribute to a feeling of unease. So, too, did the recent passing of an asteroid almost one hundred feet in diameter within thirty thousand miles of the earth.

These news stories bring to many Christians' (and others') minds apocalyptic scenarios and a lot of silly blather about the Book of Revelation (or Gog and Magog, Armageddon, the anti-Christ, the return of the Hidden Imam, and so forth). Some even understand them to be signs heralding the Rapture, when Jesus will take them directly to heaven, leaving nonbelievers standing around like wallflowers at a divine prom. A response to such events that constitutes less of a "rupture" with science and common sense is a recent abstract philosophical thought experiment. Developed by a number of people, including the Oxford philosopher Nick Bostrom and the Princeton physicist J. Richard Gott, the Doomsday argument (at least one version of it) goes roughly like this:

There is a large lottery machine in front of you, and you're told that in it are consecutively numbered balls, either 10 of them or 10,000 of them. The machine is opaque, so you can't tell how many balls are in it, but you're fairly certain that there are a lot of them. In fact, you initially estimate the probability of there being 10,000 balls in the machine to be about 95 percent and of there being only 10 balls in it to be about 5 percent.

Now the machine spins, you open a little door on its

side, and a randomly selected ball rolls out. You see that it is ball number 8, and you place it back into the lottery machine. Do you still think there is only a 5 percent chance that there are 10 balls in the machine?

Given how low a number 8 is, it seems reasonable to think that the chances of there being only 10 balls in the machine are much higher than your original estimate of 5 percent. Given the assumptions of the problem, in fact, we can use a bit of mathematics called Bayes' theorem to conclude that your estimate of the probability of 10 balls being in the machine should be revised upward from 5 percent to 98 percent. Likewise, your estimate of the probability of 10,000 balls being in it should be revised downward from 95 percent to 2 percent.

What does this have to do with Doomsday? To see, we should try to imagine a cosmic lottery machine that contains the names and birth orders of all human beings from the past, present, and future. Let's say we know that this machine contains either 100 billion names or—the optimistic scenario—100 trillion names.

And how do we pick a human at random from the set of all humans? We simply consider ourselves; we argue that there's nothing special about us or about our time and that any one of us might be thought of as a randomly selected human from the set of all humans, past, present, and future. (This part of the argument can be more fully developed.)

If we assume there have been about 80 billion humans

so far (the number is simply for ease of illustration), the first alternative of 100 billion humans corresponds to a relatively imminent end to humankind—with only 20 billion more of us to come before extinction. The second alternative of 100 trillion humans corresponds to a long, long future before us.

Even if we initially believe that we have a long, long future before us, when we randomly select a person's name from the machine and the person's birth order is only 80 billion or so, we should reexamine our beliefs. We should drastically reduce, or so the argument counsels, our estimate of the likelihood of our long survival, of there ultimately being 100 trillion of us. The reason is the same as in the example with the lottery balls: the relatively low number of 8 (or 80 billion) suggests that there aren't many balls (human names) in the machine.

Here's another slightly different example. Let's assume that Al receives about 20 e-mails per day, whereas Bob averages about 2,000 per day. Someone picks one of their accounts, chooses an e-mail at random from it, and notes that the e-mail is the fourteenth one received in the account that day. From whose account is the e-mail more likely to have come?

There are other examples devised to shore up the numerous weak points in the Doomsday argument. Some of them can be remedied, but some, in my opinion, cannot be. That even a prehistoric man (who happened to understand Bayes' theorem about probabilities) could make the same argument about a relatively imminent extinction is an objection that can at least be addressed. Inferences and assumptions about future humans and their behavior are much more problematic.

Although there's no doubt ample time to learn more about the Doomsday argument and the fishy uses of the so-called anthropic principle in philosophy, cosmology, and even everyday life, Ralph Waldo Emerson's famous existential counsel remains apt: "No man has learned anything rightly until he knows that every day is Doomsday."

In any case, stay fine-tuned.

The Ontological Argument (and Logical Abracadabra)

Ontology is the area of philosophy concerned with the abstract nature of being, and the ontological argument is one of the strangest and most logically convoluted of the arguments for the existence of God. It strikes many as a form of theological sleight of hand, a pulling of God out of a top hat. For this reason, I'll deviate from my practice of beginning with a sketch of the argument in question and instead first give something of the argument's flavor by briefly examining a few marginally related logical oddities.

One is the following dialogue found in Plato's *Euthydemus*:

DIONYSODORUS: You say you have a dog?
CTESIPPUS: Yes, a villain of one.

DIONYSODORUS: And he has puppies?

CTESIPPUS: Yes, and they are very like himself . . .

DIONYSODORUS: And the dog is not yours?

CTESIPPUS: To be sure he is mine.

DIONYSODORUS: Then he is a father, and he is yours; therefore, he is your father, and the puppies are your brothers.

This is an intentionally silly argument, but how does its logic differ from the following? Fido is a dog. Fido is yours. Therefore Fido is your dog. The same grammatical structure seems unobjectionable in the latter case. An equally flawed equivocation is expressed by the logician Raymond Smullyan, who argues: Some cars rattle. My car really is some car. So no wonder my car rattles.

The ontological argument also brings to mind paradoxes of self-reference that date back to Stoic logicians of the fourth and fifth centuries B.C.E. The oldest, best-known such paradox concerned Epimenides the Cretan, who stated, "All Cretans are liars." The crux of this so-called liar paradox is clearer if we simplify his statement to "I am lying" or, better yet, "This sentence is false." To spell this out a bit more, we'll give the label Q to "This sentence is false." Now we notice that if Q is true, then by what it says, it must be false. On the other hand, if Q is false, then what it says is true, and Q must then be true. Hence, Q is true if and only if it's false. Certainly a strange Ferris wheel of a statement!

The statement Q and variants of it are also intimately connected with some of the deepest and most important ideas in logic and philosophy and possibly even with consciousness itself. Despite this, they are often dismissed as pointless diversions, suitable only for amusing logicians and other literal-minded geeks. I must admit that on some days I feel the same way, and since this certainly is some day, I will, as a last preliminary to the ontological argument, describe the abracadabra argument for God. That is, I'll demonstrate how a relative of Q can be used to prove God's existence. Consider the two sentences below:

1. God exists.
2. Both of these sentences are false.

The second sentence is either true or false. If we assume it's true, then by what it says, both sentences are false. In particular, the second sentence is false. The only way the second sentence can be false is for the first sentence to be true. Thus in this case God exists. On the other hand, if we assume directly that the second sentence is false, then again we must note that the only way for this to be so is for the first sentence to be true. Thus in this case also God exists. Hence God exists.

Of course, in a similar way we can demonstrate that God had a hangnail or that He doesn't exist or that George W. Bush is in love with Britney Spears.

A related self-referential trick can be pulled with the following statement, which we'll symbolize by *S*.

S: "If this statement is true, then God exists."

Now let's temporarily assume that the statement *S* is true. What can we conclude from our assumption? Well, if *S* is true, then by what it says, we can conclude that God exists. You might object that we just assumed *S* was true and can't be certain of its truth. But reexamine what we have demonstrated. We've shown that if *S* is true, then God exists. But this is precisely what *S* says, and so *S* is true and God exists.

Unfortunately, the same sort of approach can be taken with the statement *T*: "If this statement is true, then God doesn't exist." This time we'd have proved that God doesn't exist.

(One resolution to these paradoxes is to be aware of the way statements can be layered. That is, we must carefully distinguish statements such as "The election was stolen" or "Henry says he's sick" from meta-statements about these statements, such as "The candidate's claim of impropriety was unfounded" or "Gertrude believes that Henry is exaggerating how bad he feels." This distinction leads us back to Russell's theory of types and everything that grew out of it and, alas, away from the matters at hand.)

. . .

Enough fun and games. Finally on to the more serious ontological argument for the existence of God, which is generally attributed to Anselm, Archbishop of Canterbury in the eleventh century. A very rough version of this argument defines God to be the greatest and most perfect possible being. It continues by assuming that this most perfect being must possess all characteristics of perfection. Since it's better to exist than not to exist, existence is a characteristic of perfection. Hence and presto, God exists by definition.

The content of this argument is easy to gloss over, so let's examine a slightly longer rendition closer to Anselm's version:

1. God is a being than which nothing greater can even be conceived.
2. We understand the notion of God as well as the notion of God's really existing.
3. Let's also tentatively assume God doesn't exist.
4. If we understand the notion of a positive being and that being really exists, then this being is greater than it would have been if we only understood the notion of it.
5. From these assumptions, we conclude that if God did not exist, we could conceive of a being greater than God (a being just like God, but really existing).

This is a contradiction since God is a being than
which nothing greater can be conceived.

6. Thus Assumption 3 is refuted and God exists.

As with some other alleged proofs for the existence of
God, this one "proves" too much. Even Gaunilo, one of
Anselm's contemporaries, notes this. Gaunilo asks us to
imagine the most perfect island conceivable, the island
than which no greater island can be conceived. The same
argument as above now demonstrates that this most perfect island must exist. (My candidate for most perfect island would be Mount Desert Island in Maine, where I'm
writing this. It's not perfect, but riding a bike along the
ocean drive with my wife or watching our daughter juggle
rubber chickens and our son make a raging campfire is
probably as close to perfect as it gets.) More generally,
variants of Gaunilo's argument can be used to "prove" the
existence of all manner of perfect entities.

Of course, someone committed to the ontological argument can reply that islands and the like are not the sorts of
things that can be perfect and ideals of perfection vary
from person to person. The abstract notion of a being, the
argument goes, does admit of absolute perfection. But does
it really? And is existence even a characteristic in anything like the same way that red or hard is?

Even the French philosopher Descartes subscribes to a
version of the ontological argument. It derives from his
conviction that he has an idea of God as a perfect being.

This idea must have as a cause something external to him since he is not perfect. Therefore, Descartes concludes, the only possible cause for his having this idea is an external perfect being, God. Only a slight caricature of Descartes's version of the ontological argument (as well as a nice twist on his "I think, therefore I am") is a paraphrase of a passage from Donald Harington's cult novel, *The Architecture of the Arkansas Ozarks*. In it someone argues, "I'm ticklish, therefore I exist"; "I can't tickle myself, therefore you exist."

Although more serious, Anselm's argument and developments and refinements of it (even that of the logician Kurt Gödel) seem to have the same level of persuasive power as the abracadabra argument mentioned above. As David Hume observed, the only way a proposition can be proved by logic and the meaning of words alone is for its negation to be (or lead to) a contradiction, but there's no contradiction that results from God's not existing.

(Relevant to further development of this idea is the well-known philosophical distinction between analytic and synthetic statements. An analytic truth is one that is true by virtue of the meanings of the words it contains, and a synthetic truth is one that is true by virtue of the way the world is. Examples include "Bachelors are unmarried men" versus "Bachelors are lascivious men" or "UFOs are flying objects that have not been identified" versus "UFOs contain little green men." When Molière's pompous doctor announces that the sleeping potion is effective because of its dormitive virtue, he is making an empty, analytic statement, not a factual, synthetic one. This analytic-synthetic distinction is a sprucing up of Immanuel Kant's original one, which in turn derives from related distinctions attributed to Hume and Gottfried Leibniz. Some philosophers, in particular the American philosopher W.V.O. Quine, have argued that the distinction is not hard and clear, but rather one of degree or convenience. It is, even if not absolute and immutable, still a useful distinction.)

Interestingly, there is a classic irreligious argument against the existence of a certain sort of God that does depend on logic and the meaning of words alone. If one assumes that God is both omnipotent and omniscient, an obvious contradiction arises. Being omniscient, God knows everything that will happen; He can predict the future trajectory of every snowflake, the sprouting of every blade of grass, and the deeds of every human being, as well as all of His own actions. But being omnipotent, He can act in any way and do anything He wants, including behaving in ways different from those He'd predicted, making His expectations uncertain and fallible. He thus can't be both omnipotent and omniscient.

The above argument notwithstanding, there is no way to conclusively disprove the existence of God. The reason is a consequence of basic logic, but is not one from which theists can take much heart. In fact, existential statements, those asserting that there is a nonmathematical entity having a certain property (or set of noncontradictory properties), can never be conclusively disproved. No matter how absurd the existence claim (there exists a dog who speaks perfect English out of its rear end), we can't look everywhere and check everything in order to assert with absolute confidence that there's no entity having the property. Existence claims can, however, be proved simply by presenting an example of an entity possessing the property in question (in this case a flatulently articulate canine pundit).

By contrast, universal statements, those asserting that every nonmathematical entity (of a given type) has a certain property (or set of noncontradictory properties), can't be conclusively proved. No matter how plausible the universal claim (all emeralds are green), we can't look everywhere and check everything in order to assert with absolute confidence that all entities (of a given type) have the property. Universal claims can, however, be disproved simply by presenting a counterexample (a red emerald), an entity that doesn't have the property in question.

So do the arguments and counterarguments in this book conclusively prove there isn't a God? No, of course not, but neither is there an argument that conclusively proves there isn't a dog who speaks perfect English out of its rear end. Nor is there a conclusive proof that there isn't a Santa, a Satan, or a Flying Spaghetti Monster (as proposed on the website www.venganza.org). Despite the vast difference in significance, gravitas, and resonance among these existence claims, they are all, by nature of their logical form, incapable of being conclusively disproved.

Finally, an apocryphal story illustrates the sometimes intimidating nature of logic and mathematics in these matters. Catherine the Great had asked the famous French philosopher Denis Diderot to her court, but was distressed to discover that Diderot was a vocal atheist. To counter him, she asked the visiting mathematician Leonhard Euler to confront Diderot. On being told that there was a new argument for God's existence, the innumerate Frenchman expressed a desire to hear it. Euler then strode forward and stated, "Sir, $\frac{(a + b^n)}{n} = x$. Hence God exists. Reply." Having no understanding of math, Diderot is reported to have been so dumbfounded he left for Paris.

I seriously doubt the story, but it is perhaps suggestive of how easily nonsense proffered in an earnest and profound manner can browbeat someone into acquiescence.

Self-Reference, Recursion, and Creation

As a brief semi-whimsical digression, I point out an interesting interplay among the notions of self-reference, recursion, creation, and some of the arguments for God. Self-referential statements I mentioned earlier in connection with a couple of well-known paradoxes. Also implicit in earlier chapters is the notion of recursion, which most naturally arises when we specify the value of a quantity in terms of its earlier values.

Slightly more precisely defined, a recursive definition of a function specifies its value at some number $(N + 1)$ in terms of its values at numbers less than or equal to N. For example, consider the mathematical factorial function, symbolized by an exclamation point (!). What is the value of 5!? It's 5 × 4! And what is 4!? It is 4 × 3!. And what is 3!? It's 3 × 2!. And what is 2!? It's 2 × 1!. Finally, what is 1!? It's just 1. This simple example notwithstanding, recursion is a very powerful idea and is indispensable to computer science. In fact, with its characteristic employment of loops—the performing of some procedure again and again for various values of some variable and the use of subroutines and other strategies for reducing complex procedures to simple arithmetical operations—recursion is at the very heart of computer programming.

The mathematical functions and algorithms that can be defined in a recursive way turn out to be precisely the ones that computers can deal with. That is, a function is recursive if and only if a computer can calculate it. (Appropriately enough, this equivalence is known as the Church-Turing thesis.) Furthermore, these recursive definitions can be nested and iterated indefinitely and, via appropriate codings and correspondences, can be extended to all sorts of activities that seem not to have much to do with computation.

The use of recursion, self-reference, and loops in some of the counterarguments for God (first cause and design, in particular) is a bit reminiscent of the following children's joke: The older child asks the younger, "Pete and Repeat were walking down the street. Pete fell down. Who was left?" The younger responds, "Repeat," to which the older comes back with, "Pete and Repeat were walking down the street. Pete fell down. Who was left?" And on and on.

Likewise, consider "Who created the Creator?" "The Creator's Creator." "And who created the Creator's Creator?" And on and on.

And to tie these ideas together, I note that creation, a divine activity, is, of course, related to reproduction, the creation of offspring. All this finally gives rise to the following sentence that, God-like (and also computer-virus-like), provides directions and raw material for its own reproduction. *Alphabetize and append, copied in quotes, these words: "these append, in Alphabetize and words: quotes, copied."*

Read the previous sentence carefully and interpret it literally. Less concisely put, it directs that the words following the colon be alphabetized and then to this alphabetized list should be appended the unalphabetized words in quotes. Presto! The sentence has reproduced itself and its descendants will do the same, and a world of sentences will proliferate.

This little riff might be taken, if you blow some theological holy smoke over it, as supplying a literal meaning to the biblical passage "In the beginning was the Word, and the Word was with God, and the word was God." Just replace the word "word" with "sentence." Yet another abracadabra argument!

Another example of creating something, the positive whole numbers, literally out of nothing is the mathematician John von Neumann's recursive definition of them. Two preliminary notions are needed: The first, the union of two sets *A* and *B*, is the set of elements in one or the other or both of the two sets. It is symbolized $A \cup B$. The second, the empty set, is the set with no elements. It is sometimes symbolized by a pair of empty braces: {}. The number 0 von Neumann simply defines to be the empty set. Then he takes the number 1 to be the union of 0 and the set containing 0. The number 2 he takes to be the union of 1 and the set containing 1, and the number 3 he takes to be the union of 2 and the set containing 2, and so on. Each number is thus the union of all its predecessors and derives ultimately from the empty set.

This is a striking example of mathematical creation ex nihilo that might easily be enlisted to support all manner of seductive nonsense. For example, God could have created the universe out of nothing in something like the way the natural numbers can be created out of nothing. In fact, much of theology, it seems to me, is a kind of verbal magic show.

A much more prosaic maneuver in religious reasoning is the hypothetical statement that seems to assert something. If such and such is the case, then this and that necessarily follow. The logic used in attempting to establish the hypothetical can be tricky, but if the assumptions are unwarranted, so are the conclusions. Apt is a well-known quotation from Bertrand Russell: "Pure mathematics consists entirely of such asseverations as that, if such and such a proposition is true of anything, then such and such another proposition is true of that thing. It is essential not to discuss whether the first proposition is really true, and not to mention what the anything is of which it is supposed to be true . . . If our hypothesis is about anything and not about some one or more particular things, then our deductions constitute mathematics. Thus mathematics may be defined as the subject in which we never know what we are talking about, nor whether what we are saying is true."

In discussing conditional statements of the above type, Russell also humorously illustrated how a false statement implies anything and, in particular, anything of a religious nature. When asked, "Do you mean that if $2 + 2 = 5$, then you are the Pope?" Russell answers affirmatively. "If we're assuming $2 + 2 = 5$, then certainly you'll agree that subtracting 2 from each side of the equation gives us $2 = 3$. Transposing, we have $3 = 2$ and subtracting 1 from each side of the equation gives us $2 = 1$. Thus since the Pope and I are two people and $2 = 1$, then the Pope and I are one. Hence I'm the Pope."

And if we began with $2 + 2 = 6$, then by the same sort of esoteric arithmetic, we could establish that $3 = 1$ and, with it, the Christian doctrine of the Trinity. This is obviously silly, but the comparable silliness of more sophisticated versions of the above is unfortunately not so apparent.

FOUR
SUBJECTIVE
ARGUMENTS

The Argument from Coincidence (and 9/11 Oddities)

James Redfield's unintentionally funny bestseller *The Celestine Prophecy* advises us to pay close attention to "strange occurrences that feel like they were meant to happen" and staunchly maintains, "They are actually synchronistic events, and following them will start you on your path to spiritual truth." The fascination with coincidences and the psychological tendency to read significance into them become for many an argument for the existence of God, for others an incitement to paranoia. This tendency is especially strong when the phenomena involved are emotionally resonant.

The schematic sketch of the argument is something like the following:

1. All these remarkable events occurring at the same time can't be an accident.
2. There must be some reason for their coincidence.
3. That reason is God.
4. Therefore God exists.

This argument is seldom made explicitly, but a number of common inane statements do more than hint at it. These statements include the perennial "Everything happens for a reason," "I don't believe in coincidence," "Their meeting that night and in that place was meant to be," and "These strange goings-on just must have a meaning." They also help explain the popularity of Redfield's book.

There are countless examples of coincidence I could use for illustration, but having mentioned emotional significance, I'll survey some of the many coincidences involving the September 11, 2001, attacks on the World Trade Center and the Pentagon. (Even for those few possibly meaningful coincidences not discussed herein, the reasons for them are no doubt prosaically human.) Another reason to focus on these paradigmatic coincidences is that the constant repetition of 9/11 has become an iconic mantra of sorts, providing an added resonance with religion.

First, there were the amateur numerologists online and elsewhere who began by pointing out that September 11 is written 9/11, the telephone code for emergencies. Moreover, the sum of the digits in 9/11 (9 + 1 + 1) is 11, September 11 is the 254th day of the year, the sum of 2, 5, and 4 is 11, and after September 11 there remain 111 days in the year. Stretching things even more, they noted that the twin towers of the WTC looked like the number 11, that the flight number of the first plane to hit the towers was 11, and that various significant phrases, including "New York City," "Afghanistan," and "the Pentagon," have 11 letters.

Less well-known is that the number 911 has a twinning property in the following rather strained sense: Take any three-digit number, multiply it by 91 and then by 11, and, lo and behold, the digits will always repeat themselves. Thus $767 \times 91 \times 11$ equals 767,767. Is this a foreboding?

There are many more of these after-the-fact manipulations, but their lesson should be clear. With a little effort, you could do something similar with almost any date or any set of words and names. The situation is analogous to the Bible codes, which I'll get to later. In the days after September 11 there were e-mails and websites claiming the Bible contains many so-called equidistant letter sequences for "Saddam Hussein" and "bin Laden," and also much longer ones describing the events of the day.

The most widely circulated of these e-mail hoaxes involved the alleged prophecies of the sixteenth-century mystic and astrologer Nostradamus. Many verses were cited, most complete fabrications. Others were variations on existing verses whose flowery, vague language, like verbal Rorschach inkblots, allows for countless interpretations. One of the most popular was "The big war will begin when the big city is burning on the 11th day of the 9th month that two metal birds would crash into two tall statues in the city and the world will end soon after." Seemingly prescient, this verse was simply made up, supermarket-tabloid-style. The truly ominous aspect of Nostradamus's *Prophecies* was that it reached the No. 1 spot on the Amazon bestseller list in the week after the attacks and that five other books about Nostradamus were in the top twenty-five. Search engines were also taxed by surfers seeking out "Nostradamus," which temporarily even beat out "adult" and "sex" in popularity.

All of these hoaxes and coincidences involved seeing or projecting patterns onto numbers and words. Photographs brought out the same tendency in some who thought they saw the "devil" in the clouds above the WTC or in the smoke coming out of it. These photos also appeared on many websites.

The reading of significance into pictures and numerical and literal symbols has a long history. Consider *I Ching* hexagrams, geometric symbols that permit an indefinitely large number of interpretations, none of which is ever shown to be correct or incorrect, accurate or inaccurate, predictive or not predictive. General numerology, too, is a very old practice common to many ancient and medieval societies. It often involves the assignment of numerical values to letters and the tortured reading of significance into the numerical equality between various words and phrases. These numerical readings have been used by

Greeks, Jews, Christians, and Muslims not only to provide confirmation of religious doctrine but also for prediction, dream interpretation, amusement, and even as aids to memory.

Of course, all people naturally search for patterns and order, but some are determined to find them whether they're there or not. Sometimes it's hard to tell whether something is significant or not. If one flips a coin many times in succession, for example, and colors the successive squares of a large checkerboard black or white depending on whether the coin lands heads or tails, the resulting randomly colored checkerboard will frequently appear to contain a representation of some sort. The tendency will be more pronounced on a three-dimensional checkerboard. But human affairs are much more multifaceted than checkerboards. There are so many ways in which numbers, names, events, organizations, and we ourselves may be linked together that it's almost impossible that there not be all sorts of meaningless coincidences and nebulous predictions. This is especially so when one is inundated with so much decontextualized information (as on the Internet) and overwhelmed by emotion.

Another property of coincidences is that they're cumulative; people remember past associations, fail to notice the many intervening disconfirming instances, and pile up examples to prove whatever they want. An illustration of the cumulative effect of the 9/11/01 coincidences moves forward a year to 9/11/02 and "demonstrates" that all major stories are connected (just as the supermarket tabloids say they are): the attacks on America in 2001, the New York State lottery, the collapse of WorldCom, the Bush administration's then just proposed war against Iraq, the death of the quarterback Johnny Unitas, and many other private events. To top this off, it seems Arthur C. Clarke, the great science fiction writer, anticipated some of these incidents decades ago.

At the perhaps considerable risk of belaboring the point, of beating a dead horse, or . . . of being repetitive, I will back up a bit. On Wednesday, September 11, 2002, the New York State lottery numbers were 911, an eerie coincidence that set many people to thinking or, perhaps more accurately, to not thinking. Once again the natural question comes to mind: How likely is this? After all, the lottery took place in New York State on the anniversary of the mass murder exactly one year before. These factors are not relevant, however. On any given day, each of the 1,000 possibilities—000, 001, . . . , 233, . . . , 714, . . . , 998, 999— is as likely to come up as any other. This is true of September 11 as well, so the probability that 911 would come up on that date is simply one in 1,000. This probability is small, but not minuscule.

The broader question that should come to mind, however, is: What is the probability that some event of this general sort—something that is resonant with the date or likely to stimulate us to think of it—would occur on September 11? The answer is impossible to say with any precision, but it is, I argue, quite high.

First off, there are two daily drawings in the New York State lottery, so there were two chances for 911 to come up that day, increasing the probability to (a bit under) one in 500. More important, there were innumerable other ways for an uncanny coincidence to occur. How many addresses or license plates, for example, have 911 in them? At each of these addresses and for each of these vehicles, something could have occurred that caused people to think of September 11. Possibilities include an accident, murder, or arrest of someone suspected of terrorism, related to a victim of the attack, or otherwise associated with it.

Or consider sports scores and statistics. There are innumerable ways for 911 to occur here. One coincidence that I personally noted involved the death of Johnny Unitas, the former Baltimore Colts star, on September 11. Arguably the best quarterback in history, he might be ranked No. 1 among NFL quarterbacks. Combine this ranking with his jersey number, 19, and you have yet another instance of 911, albeit in a different order, on September 11. You might say that there is no message associated with Unitas's death, but even those people believing in the significance of the 911 drawing can't say what its message was.

The stock market is also a major producer of numbers, many of them totally fictional. This brings to mind World-

Com, whose collapse dwarfed Enron's and whose stock was selling a bit under $64 per share at its height. The three billion or so outstanding shares are now worthless, so $191 billion in investors' wealth has disappeared. Those same three digits again! Oddly, $191 billion was very close to the Pentagon's then estimated cost for the proposed war in Iraq, which, the administration claimed (with "evidence" somewhere between dubious and trumped-up), was sheltering al Qaeda members, bringing us back once again to September 11. Talk about circular reasoning!

Another "close" example was the September 10, 2002, closing value of the September S&P 500 futures contracts. You guessed right; it was 911. And yet another lottery coincidence occurred on November 12, 2001, when 587 was drawn on the same day that Flight 587 crashed into Queens.

But once again I note that this is all too easy to do. As I've written elsewhere, the most amazing coincidence imaginable would be the complete absence of all coincidences. The above litany is intended to illustrate that there are an indeterminate number of ways for such events to come about, even though the probability of any particular one of them is tiny. And, as with creationists' probabilistic arguments, after such events occur people glom on to their tiny probability and neglect to ask the more pertinent question: How likely is something vaguely like this to occur?

Keep this in mind when you read the following excerpt from Arthur C. Clarke. In his 1973 novel *Rendezvous with*

Rama, Clarke wrote: "At 0940 GMT on the morning of September 11 in the exceptionally beautiful summer of the year 2077, most of the inhabitants of Europe saw a dazzling fireball . . . Somewhere above Austria it began to disintegrate . . . The cities of Padua and Verona were wiped from the face of the earth, and the last glories of Venice sank forever." Who would have thought that Clarke was the brains behind Osama bin Laden?

This may seem far afield from matters of (ir)religion and God's existence. But are the psychological foibles that give rise to belief in the significance of such coincidences really unrelated to some of the arguments for a belief in God? The events sketched above have many direct analogues, I maintain, in various religious traditions.

The Argument from Prophecy
(and the Bible Codes)

A theologian was lecturing on arguments for the existence of God and stated that there were exactly ten of them. A philosopher piped up from the back of the lecture hall that there were really eleven such arguments. The lecturer ignored him and continued his talk by reiterating that there were exactly ten arguments for the existence of God, but the philosopher again exclaimed that there were eleven such arguments. Persevering, the theologian proceeded by saying that the first argument for the existence of God was the argument from biblical prophecy. The philosopher called out, "Oh, I forgot about that one. I guess there are twelve."

Though held in low esteem by philosophers, the argument from prophecy is the following:

1. A holy book makes prophecies.
2. The same book or adherents of it report that these prophecies have come true.
3. The book is indubitable and asserts that God exists.
4. Therefore God exists.

Psychics, too, make all sorts of predictions, and some, of course, also come true, which is no reason to believe that psychics have access to some divine authority. Likewise, the fulfillment of holy book prophecies does not constitute a convincing argument unless the percentage of true prophecies is statistically aberrant and there are no other explanations for this aberrancy, a state of affairs for which there is no evidence.

The argument from prophecy is a special case of the argument from presupposition, roughly rendered as follows:

1. In presenting its divine narrative, a holy book presupposes God exists.
2. People read and come to accept the narrative.
3. The narrative must be true.
4. Therefore God exists.

Even after one has read a novel about a fictional character and discussed the book at length with others, it can seem odd to say that the character doesn't exist. The more details there are in a story, the more truthful the account often seems. But probabilistically speaking, the more details there are in a story, the less likely it is that the conjunction of all of them is true. Which is more likely: Congressman Smith took a bribe from a lobbyist last year, or Congressman Smith took a bribe from a lobbyist last year, took another one this year, used some of the money to rent a secret apartment for his young intern, and spent the rest of it during luxurious "fact-finding" trips with her? Despite the coherent story the second alternative begins to flesh out, the first alternative is more likely. For any statements *A*, *B*, and *C*, the probability of *A* is always greater than the probability of *A*, *B*, and *C* together, since whenever *A*, *B*, and *C* all occur, *A* occurs, but not vice versa.

Embedding God in a holy book's detailed narrative and building an entire culture around this narrative seem by themselves to confer a kind of existence on Him. Holidays, traditions, ideals, cultural identities, as valuable as they might occasionally be, all seem to add to the unwarranted presuppositions underlying them. Their familiarity also serves to inure us to the vindictive, petty, and repellent aspects of the God character.

Suspend disbelief for long enough and one can end up believing. Needless to observe, I hope, is that writing about a character isn't sufficient to conjure up his or her existence. Statements or expressions can have a meaning yet lack a referent. Bertrand Russell's celebrated "The present King of France is bald" is an example. Russell took it to mean "There is a single person who is King of France and that person is bald." On this analysis the statement is meaningful but false and doesn't imply there is a present king of France. A more germane example is "God created all the plants and animals," which should be taken to mean "There is an entity, God, and that entity created all the plants and animals." The latter is also a meaningful but false statement.

You would think that the obvious irreligious objection would come to almost anyone's mind when reading a religious tome or holy book. What if you don't believe the holy book's presuppositions and narrative claims and simply ask for independent argument or evidence for God's existence? What if you're not persuaded by the argument that God exists because His assertion that He exists and discussion of His various exploits appear in this book about Him that believers say He inspired?

If I'm impertinent enough to utter a skeptical word while people are discoursing on God or religion, they often point to the Bible (or Koran or other comparable tome) and its details, prophecies, and revelations. But pointing to some bit of biblical history or esoteric theology of which I'm not aware does not provide any reason for me to believe the claims in the Bible. Similarly, my inability to cast horoscopes or draw up sun charts does not provide any reason for me to believe in the claims of astrology. If I persist with a different issue, believers usually repeat that "it's in the Bible" and act as if the matter were therefore closed. (Reminds me of the bumper sticker that said, "God said it, I believe it, and that settle's it." A telling apostro-

phe.) Sometimes such people, admittedly not the most sophisticated of believers, resort to the argument from red
face and loud voice, an argument as difficult to refute as it
is to formulate. They bear out the aphorism about fanatics
doubling their efforts when support for their positions is
halved. Because proponents of the huff-and-puff argument repeat it incessantly, I'll repeat that claiming that a
holy book's claims are undeniable because the book itself
claims them to be is convincing only to the convinced.

(I note that testimony that someone is telling the truth
is self-undermining if the likelihood of truth-telling is less
than ½. If people are confused, lying, or otherwise deluded more often than not, then their expressions of support for each other are literally less than worthless. Imagine
for the sake of a simplistic but explicit example that some
people tell the truth ¼ of the time, lie or are mistaken ¾
of the time, and mix up their truths and falsehoods randomly. Assume that Alice and Bob are both of this type
and that Alice makes a statement. The probability that it
is true is, by assumption, ¼. Then Bob backs her up and
affirms that Alice's statement is true. Given that Bob supports it, what is the probability that Alice's statement is
true now?

You may want to skip to the last sentence of this para-
graph, or you might first ask how probable it is that Alice
utters a true statement and Bob makes a true statement of
support. Since they both tell the truth ¼ of the time, these
events will both turn out to be true $\frac{1}{16}$ of the time [¼ × ¼].

Now we ask how probable it is that Bob will make a statement of support. Since Bob will utter his support either
when both he and Alice tell the truth or when they both
say something false, the probability of this is $^{10}/_{16}$ [$^1/_4 \times ^1/_4 +$
$^3/_4 \times ^3/_4$]. Thus the probability that Alice is telling the truth
given that Bob supports her is $^1/_{10}$—the ratio of $^1/_{16}$ to $^{10}/_{16}$.
The moral: Confirmation of a person's unreliable statement
by another unreliable person makes the statement even
less reliable.)

A mathematical variant of the arguments from prophecy
and coincidence is the argument from the Bible codes.
(There are similar numerological contentions involving the
Koran and other holy books, as well as many other mathe-
matically flavored religious oddities, including a concoction
of my own available at www.math.temple.edu/paulos/
bibhoax.html.) The latest attempt to read hidden significance into the Bible began when a paper in a statistical
journal seemed to suggest that the Torah, the first five
books of the Bible, contained many so-called equidistant
letter sequences, or ELS's, that foretold significant relations
among people, events, and dates.

An ELS is an ordered set of letters, Hebrew in this case,
each letter but the first following its predecessor by a
fixed number of other letters. (The letters of the text are
run together and the spaces between words ignored.) A
simple example in English is the word "generalization,"

which contains an ELS for "Nazi"—"geNerAliZatIon"—in which the interval between letters is only of length 2. Commonly, the intervals between letters in ELS's are much longer, say, 23, 47, 69, or 92 letters long, or longer. The paper found that ELS's of (some variants of) the names of famous rabbis who lived centuries after biblical times and the ELS's of their birthdays or other related events were often close together in the Torah text and that the likelihood of this was minuscule.

The publication of the paper was viewed by the journal's editors as a mathematical conundrum: What's behind this apparent anomaly? This wasn't how the paper was viewed, however. People of various persuasions heralded this "evidence" as they had many previous Christian and Islamic numerological findings and took it to be proof of the divine inspiration of the Torah. Michael Drosnin's international bestseller *The Bible Code* went much further, even claiming to find Torah prophecies for many contemporary figures and events.

Once the discovery of seemingly prescient sequences of letters is brought to our attention, it is only natural for us to wonder about the probability of their occurrence. If we assume as a first approximation that the letters of the Torah (or any other body of text in any language) are distributed with some known frequency, the probability of observing, let's say, four letters in any given sequence of equidistant letter positions within it is easily computed. All that is required is to multiply the probabilities of occurrence of each of the four letters in the sequence. (If, for example, the language is English, then in any given position the probability of an *l* is 3.9 percent, of an *i* is 6.8 percent, of an *f* is 2.2 percent, and of an *e* is 12.4 percent, and so the probability that the four letters in "life" appear in any four given positions is simply $.039 \times .068 \times .022 \times .124$, or approximately .0000072.) The product of these four small numbers—let's call it P—is a tiny probability. Longer ELS's would be very much more improbable.

Because this likelihood is so small, we might think that the occurrence of an ELS for "life" at some particular set of positions within any text is an extraordinary event, but we must be careful about our understanding of this extreme improbability. The meaning is this: if we were to choose one text from similar texts, and if we were to designate an ordered list of four particular letter positions and then check to see if the letters were in these designated positions, the probability is P that they would be.

This procedure does not reflect, however, the way the "life" ELS was discovered. In our probability calculation we assumed that the letter sequence and positions were specified *beforehand* and the text selected and observed *afterward*. In the actual discovery of the code, however, the observation came first. That is, the "life" ELS was found, as were other related ones nearby in the document, by, we can imagine, a diligent biblical scholar. Once the sequences were found in this way, the question of the likelihood of their occurrence became moot.

Another equally salient point is that the ELS's need not occur in some particular place in the text. We're not especially concerned that a sequence begin at, say, the 14,968th letter; rather, we look for this pattern beginning *anywhere* in the text. That is, we look at all the many different letter positions in which an ELS pattern can begin (assume there are X such letter positions within the text) to see if we can find at least one instance of it. The probability of observing "life" is now considerably larger, roughly equal to $P \times X$.

Next suppose that we do not search merely for an interval of, say, 76 letters between the letters in "life," but rather search for the pattern at all possible intervals between, say, 1 and 1,000 letters and beginning anywhere in the text. With this procedure the numbers change again. The probability that we observe the pattern is approximately equal to $P \times X \times 1,000$, and this number is not so amazingly small.

And we can again increase the probability of finding such a sequence by further expanding the number of ways in which it might occur. We might allow backward searches, or look along diagonal lines in the text, or, as is the case with the Bible codes, permit distinct ELS's for the two related terms to be nearby but separated in the text, or search for alternative names and characterizations, or loosen the constraints in indefinitely many other ways.

Now, if our search for these sequences isn't conducted openly, if the cases in which we find nothing appropriate are discarded (nearby ELS's for "zucchini" and "squash," for example), if we go public only with the interesting sequences we do find, and if we compute probabilities in a simplistic way, then it is clear that these sequences do not mean what they may seem to mean on the surface. Performing a procedure one way and computing a probability associated with a different procedure is, to put it mildly, misleading. The real question isn't about the likelihood of *particular* ELS's appearing at particular positions in the text, but rather about the likelihood of *some* ELS's of vaguely similar significance appearing *somewhere* or *somehow* in the text.

Not surprisingly, when people look for ELS's in different texts, they find them. In the standard English translations of *War and Peace*, for example, there are nearby ELS's for "Jordan," "Chicago," and "Bulls," no doubt proving Tolstoy's basketball clairvoyance.

Almost all of the codes found in holy books, whether from Jewish, Christian, Islamic, or modern sources, have defects similar to those of the Bible codes. The statistical paper mentioned earlier in this chapter may also illustrate a different, more subtle defect having to do with unintentional biases in the choice of sought-after sequences, vaguely defined procedures, the variety and contingencies of ancient Hebrew spelling and variant versions of the Torah, or even Ramsey's theorem, a deep mathematical result about the inevitability of order in any sufficiently long sequence of symbols.

Common sense underscores the inanity of basing any spiritual judgments on these contextless numerological oddities.

Incidentally, I chose "life" as my illustrative ELS, since the points made above are not unrelated to the creationists' probabilistic arguments against evolution mentioned earlier.

An Anecdote on Emotional Need

I was in a beach town in Thailand on Christmas Day, 2006, and passed a rather remote Internet café where three girls were giggling and periodically running up to one or another of the ten or so computers in the room. After checking my e-mail briefly, I noticed there were Webcams on all the computers. At intervals the cameras snapped pictures of the young women, who were sending instant messages in quick succession to nine lovesick and lonely *farangs* (Thai for foreigners) around the world mooning for their "true loves" at Christmas. Apparently the men, who all appeared middle-aged, had met the girls on earlier visits to Thailand. When new pictures of their admirers appeared on the monitors, the girls would all laugh, and the English "expert" among them would write something endearing and ultimately money-extracting to each of them. The three girls would then quickly move on to another of their *sameys* (Thai for boyfriends or husbands).

Seeing my interest, they occasionally asked me what certain words in the e-mails meant. I explained that "pine for you" meant "miss you," "obsessed with you" meant "think about you all the time," and so on. Then they asked me what else they could say, so I coached them a bit, and my lines got good responses from their *sameys*, causing them to laugh uproariously. They thanked me and pumped me for more good lines, which I happily provided for quite some time. In one form or another, most promised bliss in Thailand in 2007.

It was great fun helping them dupe *farangs* on three continents out of their money via a Western Union office down the block. (Perhaps "dupe" is the wrong word since I think the bargain was a fair one and inexpensive at that: a Christmas fantasy for a few dollars.) I recalled that Christopher Moore, a Bangkok-based novelist whose compelling mysteries are set in Thailand, jokingly remarked that Thai has no common word or phrase for rigid "integrity," but many for "fun" and "smiles."

This vignette may seem far removed from the topic of this book, but it serves as an apt introduction to the next two arguments about faith and miracles. The incident came to mind when I thought of the intense need that many people have to believe in a divinity. Even if they're aware of gaping holes in the arguments for God, they want to believe as badly as the *farangs* wanted to believe in their Thai girlfriends, who were, in a sense, their goddesses. I suspect that the latter also felt a bit more than their charmingly lighthearted laughter and seemingly mercenary behavior might suggest. And what of my role, which, despite my rationale above, remains slightly problematic? I was doing the opposite of what I'm attempting to do in this book. I was facilitating an illusion, albeit an emotional one with which I have more sympathy than its religio-intellectual analogue.

Is this just a roundabout and sappy way of saying that, though I don't believe in God, I do believe in love (even deluded love)? Perhaps it is. Or it might suggest there are more things in heaven and on earth (or at least on earth) than are dreamed of in my philosophy. More likely it's just a marginally relevant anecdote. In any case, the bottom line is that I don't want to scoff too much at emotional need, whether it be of love or of God. I just don't possess the latter.

468610317
046521839
7046521A3
970465213
397046521
83970465c
1,83970465
316392046
521639704
65216397U
465218347
046521639
839704652

The Argument from Subjectivity
(and Faith, Emptiness, and Self)

I simply know. I feel Him in my bones" is one form taken by the argument from subjectivity for the existence of God. The argument is simple and very prevalent, but I'll forgo providing the long and annoying case history that writers now often feel is obligatory even in straight science reporting. (As Sarah gazed out at the tranquil ocean, she thought back to her middle-school guidance counselor, who had warned her that . . .)

The argument hinted at is clearly not valid, but it is almost impossible to dislodge. I've certainly never learned how to fruitfully discuss religion with people who have beatific grins on their faces, strangely gleaming eyes, and an air of certitude about them and who respond to any logical point I make by saying that they pity me. Nor do I know how to answer e-mails about books or columns of mine from people who say they'll pray for me and, oddly, almost always begin their missives by calling me "Sir." Such fervent believers frequently take their leave with a "God bless you" that, when said in person, often sounds as sincere as the "excuuuse me" you hear when you inadvertently bump someone in a supermarket. This isn't a big problem, of course, but a smiling shrug or an insipid e-mail is the best response I've come up with.

Put into linear form, the visceral sentiment above gives rise to this version of the argument from subjectivity:

1. People feel in the pit of their stomach that there is a God.
2. They sometimes dress up this feeling with any number of unrelated, irrelevant, and unfalsifiable banalities and make a Kierkegaardian "leap of faith" to conclude that God exists.
3. Therefore God exists.

Of course, the unrelated, irrelevant, and unfalsifiable banalities do play a role. It's been my experience that, everything being equal, many people are more impressed by fatuous blather that they don't understand than by simple observations that they do. Disdaining Occam's razor, they like their explanations hirsute.

There are many variants of this sort of argument. One is the argument from fervency:

1. I believe so fervently in God.
2. This, that, and a zillion other experiences have led to my total and absolute faith in God.
3. Therefore God exists.

Another, similar argument is that from emptiness:

1. People wonder if this is all there is and ask, "What will any of my concerns matter in one thousand years?"
2. They find this prospect so depressing that they decide there must be something more.
3. This something more they call God.
4. Therefore God exists.

A perhaps snarky response to the emptiness argument is the following. To the question "What will any of my concerns matter in one thousand years?" we might, of course, react with stoic resignation. Instead, however, we might turn the situation around. Maybe nothing we do now will matter in a thousand years, but *if so*, then it also would seem that nothing that will matter in a thousand years makes a difference now, either. In particular, it doesn't make a difference now that in a thousand years, what we do now won't matter.

As I've written, I shouldn't be dismissive of this yearning for transcendence. After all, who doesn't understand the feeling? Moving from feeling to asserting is another matter, however. As they jump to their common conclusion, the arguments above remind me of nothing so much as the Sid Harris cartoon of a blackboard filled with abstruse mathematical symbols and squiggly equations. At a crucial step in the proof appear the words "Then a miracle occurs." One of the mathematicians at the board says to the other, "I think you should be more explicit here in step two."

I think it's clear that the "subjectivity arguments" above, like others considered herein, are convincing only to people who share these visceral feelings. Since my gastric juices don't incline me to the argument's conclusion nor is it at all persuasive to countless others, what else can proponents of these arguments offer? One response, which can't be summarily dismissed, is simply the example of their belief and its effect on their lives. This effect can be impressive, but certainly doesn't compel assent. Still, one shouldn't reject the insights and feelings of those with perfect pitch simply because one is tone-deaf. Or, to vary the analogy: It wouldn't be wise for the blind to reject the counsel of sighted people.

The undermining disanalogy in this response is that a sighted person's observations can be corroborated by the blind. A sighted person's directions, for example, to take eleven steps and then to turn left for eight more steps to reach the door of the building can be checked by a blind person. How can an agnostic or atheist learn anything from someone who simply claims to know there is a God?

Unlike the situation with sighted people, whose visions and directions are more or less the same, the "knowledge" that different religious people and groups claim to possess is quite contradictory. Blind people might wonder about the worth of being sighted were different sighted people to give inconsistent directions to get to the door. Instead of the directions just mentioned, say a different sighted person directed someone to take four steps, turn left for seventeen more steps and then right for six more steps to get to the same door.

Of course, there is a strong tendency among some believers to gloss over the profound differences between physical sight and "spiritual insight" and, more generally, between science and faith. Implicit in this view is the following argument:

1. Evolution and the scientific outlook constitute a worldview. Similarly, creation science and the biblical outlook constitute a worldview.
2. All worldviews are equivalent, acceptable, and true.
3. The biblical worldview implies that God exists.
4. Therefore God exists.

The unwarranted assumption of equivalence reminds me of a story related by Bertrand Russell about when he was entering jail as a conscientious objector during World

War I. The admitting clerk asked him his religion, and when Russell responded that he was an agnostic, the clerk shook his head and said he'd never heard of that religion but that all of them worship the same God.

The only thing the incompatibility of these worldviews should compel, however, is a degree of tolerance, even if it's only of the sort H. L. Mencken described. He suggested, "We must respect the other fellow's religion, but only in the sense and to the extent that we respect his theory that his wife is beautiful and his children smart." It's repellent for atheists or agnostics to personally and aggressively question others' faith or pejoratively label it as benighted flapdoodle or something worse. Those who do are rightfully seen as arrogant and overbearing. It's been my experience, at least in this country, that it is more likely to be the religious who personally and aggressively question atheists' and agnostics' lack of faith or pejoratively label it as secular autism or worse. The latter questioning and labeling seem especially arrogant and overbearing since there is no compelling argument for the existence of a God. (This doesn't seem to prevent the frequent citation of benighted bigotry, ranging from cursing of the "infidels" to Psalms 14:1, "Fools say in their hearts, 'There is no God.' Their deeds are loathsome and corrupt, and not one does what is right.")

Furthermore, even if there were such an argument for theism, what would follow from it? Not much, since there certainly are no universal rational arguments for the long

lists of specific divine injunctions associated with particular religions and sects. It's hard even to imagine what such
an argument for, say, some sort of constraint on diet or
beard length would even look like. Still, although the
irreligious would disagree with these injunctions, most
would, I suspect, have no real quarrel with people who
simply choose to believe in some sort of nebulous higher
power (the more nebulous the better). They would likely,
however, be distinctly unimpressed by those people, sometimes quite eminent, who continue to try to forge an argument bridging theism and a particular faith. The Christian
geneticist Francis Collins tries to do this in his *Language of
God*, but one needn't be a crack logician to recognize that
belief in the divinity of Jesus simply does not follow from
belief in God. Nor does it follow from the beauty of frozen
waterfalls, as he rather amazingly claims.

I've often wondered why adherents of a particular religion and its associated figures and narratives claim to be
incapable of understanding atheists and agnostics. As has
often been noted, they generally have some relevant experience that they can call on. Their religion teaches them
to deny the figures, even the God(s), of other faiths and
traditions—Zeus, Osiris, Woden, and so on. Atheists and
agnostics simply do them one better, extending this denial
one God further to make it universal.

Subjective arguments for God's existence generally claim
to establish even more than a connection between God and
a particular religion. They claim to establish the existence

of a personal God who cares about us individually, listens to our prayers, and occasionally intervenes with a miracle on our behalf. An understandable wish perhaps, but absurd nonetheless. (Relevant is Ambrose Bierce's definition of "pray"—"to ask that the laws of the universe be annulled in behalf of a single petitioner confessedly unworthy.") At the very least this conception of God suggests a rather overweening sense of self and its importance. My own feeling derives in part from the realization, mentioned in the preface, that I had when I was ten years old and wrestling with my brother on the floor of my family's house in Milwaukee, Wisconsin. In an important sense, I mused, there was no essential difference between me and not-me; everything was composed of atoms and molecules, and though their patterns differed, the rug below our heads and the brains inside them were made of the same stuff.

This preadolescent reverie grew into an awareness that the notion of self may be a sort of conceptual chimera. Doubt that God exists is almost banal in comparison to the more radical doubt that we exist, at least as anything more than nominal, marginally integrated entities having convenient labels like "Myrtle" and "Oscar." This is, of course, Hume's idea—and Buddha's as well—that the self is an ever-changing collection of beliefs, perceptions, and attitudes, that it is not an essential and persistent entity, but rather, as stated, a conceptual chimera. Am I really the same person, for example, as the kid who would wear wide-cuffed pants whenever we had scrambled eggs in order to have somewhere to hide the hated yellow food? And am I still the person who long ago would stay up late on summer nights to watch reruns of the corny *Whirlybirds* TV series with my other brother?

Not only does the admonition "Love thy neighbor as thyself" become problematic if the notion of "self" loses its integrity, but if this belief about the ephemeral nature of selves ever became widely and viscerally felt throughout a society—whether because of advances in neurobiology, cognitive science, philosophical insights, or whatever — its effects on that society would be incalculable. Or so this assemblage of beliefs, perceptions, and attitudes sometimes thinks.

The Argument from Interventions
(and Miracles, Prayers, and Witnesses)

It was a miracle from God!" How many times have we heard such exclamations? The argument from miracles is an argument for the existence of a God that depends for whatever force it claims to have on the testimony of witnesses. The "miracles" these witnesses describe are intended to show the intervention of, and hence the existence of, a God.

1. Whether brought about by prayer or taking place spontaneously, a miracle occurs.
2. This is evidence of a divine intervention.
3. Therefore God exists.

It sometimes seems to me that news coverage of these miracles is more extensive than coverage of scientific breakthroughs. Popular accounts of miracles (as well as of mysterious prophecies) have always appeared in supermarket tabloids, where they're almost as common as unhappy celebrities. In recent years, however, they've surfaced in magazines, newspapers, and periodicals of all types, on radio and TV, and in books and movies. Studies report that a large majority of Americans of diverse religious persuasions believe in miracles.

Two weighty miracle stories, in particular, received a lot of attention in Philadelphia, my hometown. Since they provide a convenient prism through which to examine the concept of a miracle, let me very briefly describe each (although other stories would do) and then make some general remarks about miracles and related matters.

The first concerns Mother Drexel, a Philadelphia heiress, nun, and social worker who died in 1955. Nearly fifty years later she was coming to the end of the long process whereby a person is canonized a saint. The process hinged upon official certification, completed only a few months before, of two posthumous miracles that had been attributed to her. Both involved the unexplained cures of sick children.

The better-known Fátima story dates from 1917. Three peasant children in the small Portuguese village of Fátima were said to have witnessed a sequence of miraculous visions of the Virgin Mary during which she revealed to them three prophecies. The first two were long ago interpreted as foretellings of World War II and the rise and fall of Soviet Communism. The final one was said to have fore-told the shooting of Pope John Paul II.

That Mother Drexel was an admirable, compassionate, and selfless woman who divested herself of her consider-able fortune and made the world a better place I have little doubt. Nor do I have reservations about the sincerity of the Portuguese children or the piety of their many devo-tees. It's with the general notion of miracle that I have dif-ficulty, to put it mildly.

What does the word mean? If a miracle is simply a very unlikely event, then miracles occur every day. Just ask any lottery winner or bridge player. Any particular bridge hand of thirteen cards has a probability of one in 600 bil-lion of being dealt. It would nevertheless be beyond silly to look at the thirteen cards dealt to you and proclaim them to be a miracle or, worse, say that the hand's very im-probability was evidence that you were not really dealt it. Even our specific, personal genetic makeup is an extremely improbable accident. A different sperm might have united with the same or different egg, and we wouldn't have been. Still, the explanation for our personal genetic makeup de-pends on the particular sperm and egg that did, however improbably, unite.

So far, no problem. But if a miracle is intended to indi-cate that some sort of divine intervention has occurred, some questions should come to mind. Why, for example, do so many in the media and elsewhere refer to the rescu-ing of a few children after an earthquake or a tsunami as a miracle when they attribute the death of perhaps hundreds of equally innocent children in the same disaster to a geophysical fault line? It would seem either both are the result of divine intervention or both are a consequence of the earth's plates shifting.

The same irreligious point holds for other tragedies. If a recovery from a disease is considered a miraculous case of divine intervention, to what do we attribute the contracting of the disease in the first place? None except the most unenlightened maintain that AIDS is some sort of divine retribution. Alternatively put, why is it not termed a miracle when a parapet suddenly cracks at 3:06 a.m. and falls on the head of the only person walking on the street below or when a television evangelist lays his hands on a wheelchair-bound man who then goes into convulsions?

In the Mother Drexel case, two very sick children prayed to her years after she died, and they soon enjoyed spontaneous and unexplained recoveries. But such recuperations do sometimes occur, as do the more common spontaneous and unexplained deteriorations. Not knowing what causes them in every case does not mean they're instances of divine intervention. In fact, scientists are frequently unable to ascribe a specific cause to either the contracting of a disease or the recovery from it. Even statistical tests and clinical trials conducted not on one or two people but on large samples of people are sometimes insufficient to determine likely causes.

One can make similar remarks about the Fátima case.

There one should observe as well that the prophecies were so vague that many different interpretations might have been given to them. It's not particularly risky to predict that wars and mayhem will occur at some indefinite time in the future. If one really wanted to investigate the validity of prophecies, one would need predictions that were more precise and a bit more falsifiable, and one would need to establish strict protocols for investigating them.

Likewise, if one really wanted to search for a causal connection between prayers and cures, one would need to examine a very large number of cases, set time limits on the alleged cures, compare recovery rates of those who pray with rates of those who don't, and guard against self-deception and wish fulfillment. In all these cases, believers always have an out in the "God of the gaps," whose performance of miracles, although consistent with natural laws, exploits the ever-decreasing gaps in our scientific knowledge. As Einstein noted, however, this approach is too easy: "To be sure, the doctrine of a personal God interfering with natural events could never be refuted . . . for this doctrine can always take refuge in those domains in which scientific knowledge has not yet been able to set foot."

Another related and serious conceptual problem with proclaiming a miracle was noted a long time ago by David Hume. He wrote, "A miracle is a violation of the laws of nature; and as a firm and unalterable experience has established these laws, the proof against a miracle, from the very nature of the fact, is as entire as any argument from experience can possibly be imagined." That is, the whole weight of science is the prima facie evidence against a miracle's having occurred. Carl Sagan's remark "Extraordinary claims require extraordinary evidence" is germane and, incidentally, can be formalized by a use of Bayes' theorem. This doesn't mean scientific laws are always correct. Whatever evidence exists that a certain phenomenon miraculously violates a particular scientific law is evidence as well that the scientific law in question is simply wrong. If before the invention of the telephone, for example, someone heard the voice of a friend who was hundreds of miles away, one might consider this a miracle. The evidence for this miraculous event, however, would also be evidence that the physical law that the event appears to violate (regarding how fast sound travels in air, let's say) is wrong or doesn't apply.

And about the testimony of witnesses Hume wrote, "No testimony is sufficient to establish a miracle unless the testimony be of such a kind that its falsehood would be more miraculous than the fact which it endeavors to establish." What's more likely, that a distraught mother was lying, deluded, or mistaken or that her hopelessly ill child made a spontaneous and miraculous recovery?

It's become somewhat fashionable to say that religion and science are growing together and are no longer incompatible. This convergence is, in my opinion, illusory. In fact, I don't believe that any attempt to combine these very disparate bodies of ideas can succeed intellectually. This is not to say, of course, that religious and irreligious people cannot respect each other's struggle to make sense of the world.

In any case, whatever the causes of their remarkable recoveries, even the irreligious can be secularly glad that the two children who prayed to Mother Drexel have completely recuperated and that Pope John Paul survived long past the assassination attempt on him. The recent effort of religious authorities to concoct a miracle that can be attributed to Pope John Paul in order to expedite his sainthood cannot, however, be so universally applauded.

The resort to dreams, premonitions, absurd connections, and posthumous interventions in the argument from miracles is irrational, but it's not honestly so, as is the surrealists' two-word argument for God. Their argument: Pipe cleaner.

Remarks on Jesus and Other Figures

Over its lengthy run, Mel Gibson's movie *The Passion of the Christ* elicited countless reactions from Catholics, Jews, fundamentalist Christians, and others. Millions of viewers contributed to its hundreds of millions of dollars in gross earnings, and film critics and cultural commentators of all persuasions weighed in on it in large numbers. Jesus is crucial to many Christians' belief in God, and aspects of his story apply as well to Moses, Muhammad, (some accounts of) Buddha, and a number of other prophets, teachers, avatars, and martyrs. For these reasons the movie is a convenient point of departure for discussing some issues of relevance to the primary topic of this book. After all, these figures are often themselves taken by many as proofs of God's existence.

My first observation is that even about modern-day mega-news stories we're often clueless. A bit more than forty years ago, in the full glare of the modern media, John F. Kennedy was assassinated, and we have only a hazy idea of the motivation of the killer or, possibly, killers. And a bit more than thirty years ago, the Watergate controversy erupted before a phalanx of cameras and microphones, and we still don't know who ordered what. And only a few years ago, well into the age of the Internet, the World Trade Center and the Pentagon were attacked, the United States responded by invading Iraq, and we have yet to learn the complete story of the attack, the training of the attackers, the lead-up to the war, and so on.

These (and many, many other) examples of our ignorance of the details of recent events don't seem surprising. We're accustomed to suspending judgment, to estimating probabilities. We realize that people dissemble, spin, exaggerate, and misinterpret. And we know that even more frequently events transpire with no witnesses, and so we've developed an appropriate skepticism about news stories and opinion pieces.

But such skepticism sometimes deserts people when they consider more distant historical happenings. This attitude is very odd, since historians are subject to even more severe limitations than those facing contemporary journalists and writers. After all, printing presses and computers haven't been around that long, but hearsay and unreliable narrators have been (or so someone told me).

As noted, the occasion for these observations is Gibson's gory movie and an underreported fact about its basis: there is little, if any, external historical evidence for the details presented in the somewhat inconsistent biblical versions of the Crucifixion. Unless we take literally and on faith the New Testament accounts of Jesus written many decades afterward (between 70 and 100 C.E.), we simply don't know what happened almost two millennia ago, at least in any but the vaguest way. This, of course, is part of the reason that Dan Brown's *The Da Vinci Code*, which purports to fill in the details of the story and its aftermath, was No. 1 on Amazon for so long, selling millions of copies to date.

Let's put aside the obvious biological absurdities of Jesus' virgin birth and resurrection (events whose truth is unquestioned by 80 percent of Americans) and focus instead on the political situation at the time. Assume for the moment that compelling historical documents have just come to light establishing the movie's and the Bible's contentions that a group of Jews was instrumental in bringing about the death of Jesus; that Pilate, the Roman governor, was benign and ineffectual; and so on. Even if all this were the case, does it not seem hateful, not to mention un-Christian, to blame contemporary Jews? Blame is all the more inappropriate if Jesus' suffering is, as many Christian theologians claim, a condition for others' being saved.

We can gain a little perspective by comparing the Crucifixion of Jesus with the killing of another ancient teacher, Socrates—the Passion of the Christ versus the Poisoning of Socrates, if you will. Again the standard story is somewhat problematic, but even if we give full credit to Plato's twenty-four-hundred-year-old account of Socrates' death, what zealous coterie of classicists or philosophers would hold today's Greeks responsible?

To ask the question is to dismiss it. It would be absurd, not to mention un-Socratic, for anyone to attribute guilt to contemporary Athenians. (Incidentally, Socrates needs a Mel Gibson or Dan Brown; sadly, the Amazon rankings of the various editions of *The Trial and Death of Socrates* range from poor to abysmal.) The case of Socrates suggests another comparison. Would a cinematic account of his death focus unrelentingly on his clutching his throat and writhing in agony on the ground after drinking the hemlock? Would such an imagined film's moving cinematography and its actors speaking in archaic Greek do anything at all to increase the likelihood that the events really occurred as depicted?

Whatever one's beliefs or lack thereof, Socrates and Jesus (at least as portrayed by Plato and the authors of the New Testament) were great moral leaders whose ideas constitute a good part of the bedrock of our culture. Their lives and teachings as they've come down to us are, in my avowedly secular opinion, more important than the details of their deaths, which are likely to remain nebulous at best.

Two peripheral points involving Jesus. The first involves the Christian writer C. S. Lewis's book *Mere Christianity* and his related public talks, which took exception to those who call Jesus a great moral teacher but not divine. He asked whether Jesus was "a liar, a lunatic, or the Lord." Citing biblical passages where Jesus says he's the Son of God, Lewis maintained that if Jesus were a manipulative liar or a deluded lunatic, he would not be much of a moral teacher. Thus anyone who calls him a moral teacher must reject these two possibilities and acknowledge him to be the Lord.

Aside from its alliteration, Lewis's question is not compelling in the least. Did Jesus really say he was the Son of God? We don't know. Could he have meant it metaphorically rather than literally? We don't know. Could he be an amalgam of various real and mythic figures? We don't even know this. (Such untestable speculations about Jesus and other figures remind me of the classics scholar who published a seminal breakthrough. The *Iliad* and the *Odyssey* were not written by Homer, he asserted. They were actually written by another blind Greek poet of the same name.) In any case, there are many ways out of this trilemma that commit one neither to abandoning admiration for (at least a good chunk of) Jesus' teaching nor to accepting his divinity.

The second point involves the aforementioned *Da Vinci Code*, which is based on the premise that Jesus married and had children and that a single direct descendant of his is alive today. Probability theory tells us, however, that if

Jesus had any children, his biological line would almost certainly have either died out after relatively few generations or else grown exponentially, so that many millions of people alive today would be direct descendants of Jesus.

Perhaps surprisingly, this is not a special trait of Jesus' possible descendants. If Julius Caesar's children and their descendants had not died out, then many millions of people alive today could claim themselves Caesar's descendants. The same can be said of the evil Caligula and of countless anonymous people living two thousand years ago. It isn't impossible to have just a few descendants after two thousand years, but the likelihood is less than minuscule.

The research behind these conclusions, growing out of a subdiscipline of probability theory known as branching theory, is part of the work of Joseph Chang, a Yale statistician, and Steve Olson, author of *Mapping Human History: Genes, Race, and Our Common Origins*. A feel for the result can be obtained by realizing that everyone has two parents, four grandparents, eight great-grandparents, sixteen great-great-grandparents, and, in general, 2^N ancestors at the Nth previous generation. If we go back just forty generations, less than a thousand years, everyone alive today would have a trillion ancestors, far, far more than the population of the world now, much less then. The only resolution is to realize that these trillion people were not distinct individuals. Back then, your ancestors and mine, as well as George Bush's, Osama bin Laden's, Oprah Winfrey's, Mao

Tse-tung's, Albert Einstein's, and the Maytag repairman's, were all pretty much the same people.

Going back three thousand years to 1000 B.C.E., we can state something even more astonishing. If anyone alive then has any present-day descendants, then we would all be among them. That is, we are descended from all the Europeans, Asians, Africans, and others who lived three thousand years ago and who have descendants living today. Consider the implications for future generations. If you have children and if your biological line doesn't die out, then every human being on earth roughly three thousand years from now would be your direct descendant.

Getting back to *The Da Vinci Code*, we can conclude that if the heroine of the book were indeed descended from Jesus, then she would share that status with many millions, if not billions, of other people as well. This makes the book's plot even harder to swallow, but then probability was never much of a match for fiction or Hollywood or, for that matter, biblical claims. Yet another problem with the virgin birth of the human Jesus is the source of his DNA, his Designer Genes, if you will, but that's a bit too peripheral to my focus here.

Many important stories of the recent past contain large holes and blank spots, and those of the distant past even larger ones. Publicly expressing disbelief or at least acknowledging uncertainty about them requires, to return to Gibson, a braver heart than denying them.

FOUR
PSYCHO-
MATHEMATICAL
ARGUMENTS

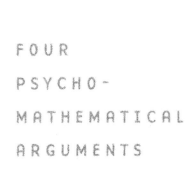

The Argument from Redefinition
(and Incomprehensible Complexity)

Many different arguments for the existence of God redefine Him to be something else. Pantheistic approaches often take God to be synonymous with life, nature, or existence. Some thinkers such as Albert Einstein, Stephen Hawking, and Baruch Spinoza seem to identify Him with the laws of physics or the structure of the universe. Einstein wrote, "I have found no better expression than 'religious' for confidence in the rational nature of reality, insofar as it is accessible to human reason." Paul Erdos, the prolific Hungarian mathematician, seemed to express a similar sentiment about mathematics. Although an atheist, Erdos often referred to an imaginary book in which God has inscribed all the most beautiful mathematical proofs. Whenever he thought that a proof or argument led to a particularly exquisite epiphany, he'd say, "This one's from the book." (Alas, none of the arguments for the existence of God are even close to being in God's book.)

Of course, if one refers to or defines God in one of these nonstandard ways, then being a "religious" theist is much more intellectually palatable. Such redefinitions are, I'd like to think (but don't), part of the reason for the high percentage of people who say they are believers.

The sketch of the argument by redefinition is:

1. God is really this, that, or the other thing.
2. The existence of this, that, or the other thing is somewhat plausible, if not obvious.
3. Therefore God exists.

A more pejorative term for (some instances of) redefinition is "equivocation." One of my favorite examples of the latter, this time with a verb, is the answer given on an algebra test to the following question: Expand $(a + b)^4$. (Recall that this means to write out the product of $(a + b)$ $(a + b)(a + b)(a + b)$.) The student's response was the following sequence:

$$(a+b)^4, (a + b)^4, (a + b)^4, (a + b)^4, (a + b)^4$$

Announcing that God is Love and that you believe in Love so you believe in God is not much more compelling.

More thoughtful redefinition takes God to be the incomprehensibly complex, a redefinition that may even allow agnostics and atheists to aver that they believe in God. Who, after all, believes they understand everything? We can certainly all agree that we're finite entities capable only of processing information of quite limited complexity. In fact, a rephrasing of the logician Kurt Gödel's famous incompleteness theorem by Gregory Chaitin shows that we (or any formal system) can only generate information whose complexity is less than our (its) own. And we can't, as Chaitin has observed, prove ten-pound theorems with five pounds of axioms. The consequence is that thoroughly understanding nature and society, which are of complexity much greater than ours, is literally beyond our "complexity horizon."

Quite conceivably, the true "theory of everything," the holy grail of modern physicists, might also be beyond our collective complexity horizon. Compare Arthur C. Clarke's comment: "Any sufficiently advanced technology is indistinguishable from magic." In any case, the verbal trick of defining God as the incomprehensibly complex, a variant of the God of the gaps, has the appeal of getting something—God, in this case—for nothing.

But even about the incomprehensibly complex, we can say something. This is an idea that I've always been attracted to, that whatever the chaos in the collage of life, it's nevertheless inevitable that there will be pattern or order of some sort on some level. No universe could be completely random at all levels of analysis; no mess could be absolutely total. It's impossible that we would be unable to point to some regularity, some invariant somewhere, no matter what the jumbled details of any particular state of affairs. One could at the very least describe the mess (assuming one was around, which is not likely) or enunciate some higher-order prediction to the effect that no lower-order predictions seem to work. Since a lack of order is also a kind of higher-level order, the notion of the inevitability of order, like the notion of God as the incomprehensibly complex, is empty, vacuous, tautologous—but it is, I think, perhaps a fruitful tautology.

In physics the idea of the inevitability of order arises in the kinetic theory of gases. There, an assumption of disorder on one formal level of analysis—the random movement of gas molecules—leads to a kind of order on a higher level: the relations among macroscopic variables such as temperature, pressure, and volume known as the gas laws. The latter law-like relations follow from the lower-level randomness and a few other minimal assumptions. More generally, any state of affairs, no matter how disorderly, can simply be described as random, and, ipso facto, at a higher level of analysis we have at least one useful "meta-law": there is randomness on the lower level.

In addition to the various laws of large numbers studied in statistics, a notion that manifests a different aspect of this idea is the statistician Persi Diaconis's remark that if you look at a big enough population long enough, then "almost any damn thing will happen."

A more profound version of this line of thought can be traced to the British mathematician Frank Ramsey, who proved a theorem stating that for a sufficiently large set of elements (people or numbers or geometric points), every pair of whose members are, let's say, either connected or unconnected, there will always be a large subset of the original set with a special property. Either all of the subset's members will be connected to each other, or all of its members will be unconnected to each other. This subset is an inevitable island of order in the larger unordered set. It is the free lunch (God) guaranteed to exist if the cafeteria (universe) is large enough.

(This is sometimes phrased in terms of guests at a dinner party. The Ramsey question for the island of order 3 is: What is the smallest number of guests who need be present so that it will be certain that at least three of them will know each other or at least three of them will be strangers to each other? Assume that if Martha knows George, then George knows Martha. The answer is six, and the proof, which I'll omit, isn't difficult. For the island of order 4, the number of guests necessary is eighteen; at least eighteen guests need be present so that it will be certain there are at least four who will all know each other or at least four who will all be strangers to each other. For order 5, the number is somewhere between forty-three and fifty-five. For larger numbers, the analysis gets much more complicated, and answers to Ramsey-type questions are known for very few numbers.)

Since Ramsey died in 1930, a whole mathematical sub-discipline has grown up devoted to proving theorems of the same general form: How big does a set have to be so that there will always be some subset of a given size that will possess some regular pattern, an island of order of some sort? The aforementioned mathematician Paul Erdos discovered many such islands, some of them ethereally beautiful. The details of the particular islands are complicated, but in general the answer to the question about the necessary size of the set often boils down to Diaconis's dictum: if it's big enough, "almost any damn thing will happen." Ramsey-type theorems may even be part of the explanation for some of the equidistant letter sequences that constitute the Bible codes. Any sufficiently long sequence of symbols, especially one written in the restricted vocabulary of ancient Hebrew, is going to contain subsequences that appear meaningful.

Of more direct relevance to evolution and the origin of complexity is the work of Stuart Kauffman. In *At Home in the Universe: The Search for Laws of Self-Organization and Complexity*, Kauffman discusses "order for free," or at least complexity at a good price. Motivated by the idea of hundreds of genes in a genome turning on and off other genes and the order and pattern that nevertheless exist, Kauffman asks us to consider a large collection of ten thousand lightbulbs, each bulb having inputs from two other bulbs in the collection.

Subject only to this constraint, one connects these bulbs

at random. One also assumes that a clock ticks off one-second intervals, and at each tick each bulb goes either on or off according to some arbitrarily selected rule. For some bulbs the rule might be to go off at any instant unless both inputs are on the previous instant. For others it might be to go on at any instant if at least one of the inputs is off the previous instant. Given the random connections and random assignment of rules, it would be natural to expect the collection of bulbs to flicker chaotically with no apparent pattern.

What happens, however, is that very soon one observes order for free, more or less stable cycles of light configurations, different ones for different initial conditions. As far as I know, the result is only empirical, but I suspect it may be a consequence of a Ramsey-type theorem too difficult to prove. Kauffman proposes that some phenomenon of this sort supplements or accentuates the effects of natural selection. Although there is certainly no need for yet another argument against the seemingly ineradicable silliness of "creation science," these lightbulb experiments and the unexpected order that occurs so naturally in them do seem to provide one.

In any case, order for free and complexity greater than we possess are to be expected and are no basis for believing in God as traditionally defined. If we redefine God to be an inevitable island of order or, as Kauffman believes, some sort of emergent entity, then the above considerations show that He exists in this very strained Pickwickian sense.

The Argument from Cognitive Tendency
(and Some Simple Programs)

Innate cognitive biases and illusions are among the factors inclining people to believe in God (or, giving due weight to Mammon as well, to invest irrationally). Others, however, see these same predilections as heralding the truth. Putting this latter view into the form of an argument, we get something like the following:

1. Some cognitive tendencies suggest the existence of an all-powerful agent.
2. These tendencies and tropes are not illusions, but point to this agent's being real.
3. Therefore this agent, God, exists.

Like other arguments considered herein, this argument doesn't come close to being valid, with the jump from Assumptions 1 to 2 being unwarranted. If a mind-set is natural or innate, this doesn't mean necessarily that it is rationally defensible. Racism is an example. Still, these predilections do provide a partial explanation for why some believe as they do. As Daniel Dennett and others have noted, in seeking explanations and patterns, people have an inborn tendency to search for agents or intentions rather than accidental or impersonal causes. Moreover, they're more likely to attribute an event to an agent than to chance if it has momentous or emotional implications, and what is of more visceral importance to many than religion?

In one relevant experiment, for example, a group of subjects was told that a man parked his car on an incline, forgot to engage the emergency brake, and walked away. After his departure the car rolled downhill into a fire hydrant. Another group was given the same preamble but was told that after the man's departure, the car rolled into a pedestrian, who was badly injured. The members of the first group generally viewed the event as an accident and offered excuses for the driver. The second group held the driver responsible and was quite critical of him. Needless to say, the infraction in both cases was the same. It was an accident and the driver was responsible, but which of these two facts to emphasize was a function of the emotions aroused.

Or consider the assassination of John F. Kennedy, a heartrending event for many. Because of its momentous nature, people searched for a suitably momentous reason for the assassination. Lee Harvey Oswald was an unprepossessing nobody who seemed ill suited for the job of giant-slayer. There had to be something more, and maybe there was, but one added reason for the intense fascination with other possibilities was the charming superstition that significant consequences must necessarily be the result of significant perpetrators. Similar remarks apply to the death of Princess Diana.

Again, what has more significance than the origin of the universe, the nature of good and evil, and the other weighty issues in which religion traffics? Hence there is a natural tendency to search for an agent—God—rather than accept an accidental, impersonal, or irreligious account.

Another cognitive foible relevant to religious belief is the so-called confirmation bias, a psychological tendency to seek confirmation rather than disconfirmation of any hypothesis we've adopted, however tentatively. People notice more readily and search more diligently for whatever might confirm their beliefs, and they don't notice as readily and certainly don't look as hard for what disconfirms them. The prosecution of the unwarranted (to describe it blandly) Iraq war is a textbook example of this absurdly willful myopia and the staggering enormity of the consequences to which it can lead. Francis Bacon was aware of this bias in the seventeenth century when he wrote, "The human understanding when it has once adopted an opinion . . . draws all things else to support and agree with it. And though there be a greater number and weight of instances to be found on the other side, yet these it either neglects and despises." Considerably newer results in brain imaging have even located where in the brain confirmation bias seems to reside.

The obstinate blindness to contrary facts that confirmation bias induces in some religious people always reminds me of the little ditty by William Hughes Mearns:

> *As I was sitting in my chair,*
> *I knew the bottom wasn't there,*
> *Nor legs nor back, but I just sat,*
> *Ignoring little things like that.*

Confirmation bias also plays a role in developing religious and other harmful stereotypes. Although often useful shorthand, stereotypes can result in an initial ill-considered characterization thereafter becoming almost immune to revision. And just as confirmation bias plays an important role in stock-picking obsessions, it's relevant as well to worldview-picking obsessions, where an initial disposition to believe because of childhood training or the ambient society's prevailing ethos can become an indubitable certainty.

Related to the idea of the prevailing religious ethos is

the "availability error," another cognitive oddity described at length by the psychologists Amos Tversky and Daniel Kahneman. It is simply the inclination to view any story, whether political, personal, or religious, through the lens of a superficially similar story that readily comes to mind or is psychologically available. Thus every American military involvement is inevitably described as "another Vietnam." Political scandals are immediately compared to the Lewinsky saga or Watergate, misunderstandings between spouses reactivate old wounds, a new high-tech firm has to contend with memories of the dot-com bubble, and any story with a vaguely religious theme is elided into a familiar tale from one's own religion.

And since the God story is ubiquitous in most religions (some versions of Buddhism being a happy and notable exception), even other religions are taken as confirming the existence of God. This generally isn't enough to induce understanding of, let alone conversion to, other religions. Powerful family and group dynamics, including the aforementioned confirmation bias, ensure that most families share the same religion. Children of Baptists, Episcopalians, and Catholics usually remain so or at most switch Christian denominations. Likewise with Reform, Conservative, and Orthodox Jews, Sunni and Shiite Muslims, and other religions' denominations; there is movement perhaps between denominations, but little drift to other religions.

This phenomenon of an assumed religious inheritance and its many consequences is not necessarily "wicked" or an "abuse," as Richard Dawkins has suggested, but it does indicate that religious beliefs generally arise not out of a rational endeavor but rather out of cultural traditions and psychological tropes. The hoary argument from tradition is probably the most potent of arguments for the existence of God, specifically the God of our ancestors. Why else would children so often adhere to the same religion as their parents? To refer to Catholic children, Protestant children, or Islamic children is to assume that the children automatically inherit their parents' worldview. Although often true, this assumption isn't a necessary fact of life, and, as Dawkins has wisely noted, it might be salubrious if referring to children in this way came to sound as wrongheaded as referring to them as Marxist children or capitalist children.

The last cognitive distortion I'll discuss is a form of primitive thinking related to the availability error. It is best characterized as "like causes like." For example, doctors once believed that the lungs of a fox cured asthma and other lung ailments. People assumed that fowl droppings eliminated the similar-appearing ringworm. Freudians asserted that fixation at the oral stage led to preoccupation with smoking, eating, and kissing.

It is perhaps not surprising therefore that people have long thought the complexity of computer outputs was a result of complex programs. It's been known for a while, however, that this is not necessarily the case. Computer scientists and mathematicians, notably John von Neumann in the 1950s and John Horton Conway in the 1970s, have studied simple rules and algorithms and have observed that their consequences sometimes *appear* inordinately complex. The same is true of the famous Mandelbrot set, which is generated by a few equations. The relevance of this finding to the arguments from design and first cause is clear:

1. The world is exceedingly complex.
2. Like causes like.
3. So something very complex caused the world.
4. That cause is God, who therefore exists.

Although it's not a new idea, no one has treated the notion of simplicity leading to complexity with the thoroughness of Stephen Wolfram in his book *A New Kind of Science*. The book is twelve hundred pages, so let me focus on Wolfram's so-called rule 110, one of a number of very simple algorithms capable of generating an amazing degree of intricacy and, in theory at least, of computing anything any state-of-the-art computer can compute.

Imagine a grid (or, if you like, a colossal checkerboard), the top row of which has a random distribution of white squares and black ones. The coloring of the squares in the first row determines the coloring of the squares in the second row as follows: Pick a square in the second row, and check the colors of the three squares above it in the first row (the one above it to the left, the one immediately above it, and the one above it to the right). If the colors of these three squares are, in order, WWB, WBW, WBB, BWB, or BBW, then color the square in the second row black. Otherwise, color it white. Do this for every square in the second row.

Via the same rule, the coloring of the squares in the second row determines the coloring of the squares in the third row, and in general the coloring of the squares in any row determines the coloring of the squares in the row below it. That's it, and yet, Wolfram argues, the patterns of black and white squares that result are astonishingly similar to patterns that arise in biology, chemistry, physics, psychology, economics, and a host of other sciences. These patterns do not look random, nor do they appear to be regular or repetitive. They are, however, exceedingly complex, at least according to some but not all measures of complexity.

Moreover, if the first row is considered the input, and black squares are considered to be 1s and white ones 0s, then each succeeding row can be considered the output of a computation that transforms one binary number into another. (Note that the first row of randomly distributed white and black squares corresponds to the complexity and contingency of the initial physical conditions, while the simple rules correspond to the deterministic laws of physics.) Not only can this simple so-called one-dimensional cellular automaton perform the particular calculation just described, but, as Wolfram proves, it is capable of performing all possible calculations! It is a "universal" computer that, via appropriate codings, can emulate the actions of any other special-purpose computer, including, for example, the word processor on which I am now writing.

A number of such idealized universal computers have been studied (ranging from Turing machines through Conway's game of Life to more recent examples), but Wolfram's rule 110 is especially simple. He concludes from it and a myriad of other considerations too numerous to list here that scientists should direct their energies toward simple programs rather than equations since programs are better at capturing the interactions that characterize scientific phenomena.

Wolfram also puts forward a principle of "computational equivalence," which asserts, among other things, that almost all processes, artificial (such as his rule 110) or natural (such as those occurring in biology or physics), that are not obviously too simple can give rise to universal computers. This is reminiscent of an old theorem known as the Church-Turing thesis, which maintains that any rule-governed process or computation that can be performed at all can be performed by a Turing machine or equivalent universal computer. Wolfram, however, extends the principle, gives it a novel twist, and applies it everywhere.

Simple programs, he avers, can be used to explain space and time, mathematics, free will, and perception as well as help clarify biology, physics, and other sciences. They also explain how a universe as complex-appearing and various as ours might have come about: the underlying physical theories provide a set of simple rules for "updating" the state of the universe, and such rules are, as Wolfram demonstrates repeatedly, capable of generating the complexity around (and in) us, if allowed to unfold over long enough periods of time.

The relevance of the "like causes like" illusion to the argument from design is now, I hope, quite obvious. Wolfram's rules, Conway's Life, cellular automatons in general, and the Mandelbrot set, as well as Kauffman's lightbulb genome, show that the sources of *apparent* complexity needn't be complex (although they usually are).

My Dreamy Instant Message Exchange with God

While writing the last two chapters on the cognitive foibles of humans and the many redefinitions of God, I dreamed I had a cryptic instant message exchange with a rather reasonable and self-effacing entity who claimed to be God. This is my reconstruction of our conversation.

>   **ME:** Wow, you say you're God. Hope you don't take offense if I tell you that I don't believe in you?
>
>   **GOD:** No, that's fine. I doubt if I'd believe in me, either, if I were you. Sometimes I even doubt if I believe in me, and I am me. Your skepticism is bracing. I'm afraid I don't have much patience for all those abject believers who prostrate themselves before me.
>
>   **ME:** Well, we share that sentiment, but I don't get it. In

what sense are you God, aside from your e-mail address—god@universe.net? Are you all-powerful? All-knowing? Did you have something to do with the creation of the universe?

GOD: No, no, and no, but from rather lowly beginnings I have grown more powerful, I've come to understand more, I've emerged into whatever it is I am, and I know enough not to pay much attention to nonsensical questions about the "creation" of the universe.

ME: It's interesting that you claim to be God, yet use quotation marks to indicate your distance from the writings of some of those who believe in you.

GOD: I already told you that I'm a little tired of those people. I didn't create the universe, but gradually grew out of it or, if you like, evolved from the universe's "biological-social-cultural" nature. How about that hyphenated word for quotation marks? You might guess that the quotation marks suggest that sometimes I want to distance myself from some of my own writings.

ME: I like that you're no literalist. Any evidence of irony or humor seems to me to be a good sign. Still, I'm not sure I understand. Are you saying that you sort of evolved out of something simpler, maybe something like us humans?

GOD: I guess you could say that, except that my background is much more inclusive than that of just you humans. And looking around at what a mess you've made, I'm tempted to say, "Thank God for that," but that seems a little too self-congratulatory. Besides, you've done a lot of good things, too, and I've had my share of failure and misadventure, and I'm still learning.

ME: So, you're a bit of an underachieving comedian? And I take it you're a natural being, not a supernatural one?

GOD: Well, yes and no. I'm natural in the sense that any explanation of my provenance, existence, and slow development would be a scientific one. I'm supernatural only in the sense that I'm really rather super. That's not to say I'm super because I aspire to—excuse the term—lord it over you. It's just a straightforward statement of fact that along many dimensions (but not all) I've come to a greater understanding of things than you yet have. So it might be more accurate to say I'm relatively super.

ME: Relatively super, but still a relative. A bit mightier, but not almighty. Right?

GOD: Those are nice ways of putting it.

ME: And believers? As relatively super, you probably see them as pretty ignorant, maybe something like the cargo cultists of the Pacific, picking things to worship without any sort of natural context or much real understanding.

GOD: No, I'm more kindly disposed toward them than

that. In fact, I love the poor benighted "souls." That last word is intended figuratively, of course.

ME: I'm still confused. Are you, despite being a bit mightier, ever confused about things? Are you ever torn in different directions, not completely certain?

GOD: Oh my God, yes. I'm regularly confused, torn, and uncertain about all manner of things. I can't measure up to all that perfect-God stuff. Makes me feel inferior. Whatever was that Anselm thinking? For example, I wish I could constrain the most superficially ardent of my believers and tell them to cool it. Look around and think a bit. Marvel at what you've come to understand and endeavor to extend this scientific understanding. Then again I think, No, they have to figure this out for themselves.

ME: If you're as knowledgeable as you claim, why don't you at least explain to us lower orders the cure for cancer, say.

GOD: I can't do that right now.

ME: Why not? You can't intervene in the world?

GOD: Well, the world is very complicated, so I can't do so yet in any consistently effective way. Still, since I'm actually a part of the world, any future "interventions," as you call them, would be no more mysterious than the interventions of a wise anthropologist on the people he studies, people who in turn might influence the anthropologist. Nothing miraculous about entities affecting each other. Nothing easy about predicting the outcomes of these interactions, either, which is why I'm hesitant about interfering.

ME: You've declared you're advanced in many ways, but do you claim to be unique? Do other "Gods" or other "a bit mightiers" a bit mightier than you exist? Do other "super universes" exist? See, I can use quotation marks, too. And where are you? In space? Inherent in other sentient beings? Part of some sort of world-brain?

GOD: Not sure what questions like these even mean. How do you distinguish beings or universes? And in what sense do you mean "exist"? Exist like rocks, like numbers, like order and patterns, or maybe like the evanescent bloom of a flower? As I said, I'm not even sure I'm God, nor would I swear that you aren't. Maybe God is our ideals, our hopes, our projections, or maybe you humans are all super-simulations on some super yearn engine like God-gle.

ME: The Matrix, the dominatrix, the whatever. Hackneyed, no? Anyway, even if you do exist in some sense, and I'm not buying that, you're certainly nothing like God as conventionally conceived. Do you think there is a God of that sort?

GOD: I know of no good evidence or logical argument for one.

ME: I agree there, but I also suspect most people would find you a pretty poor substitute for that God.

GOD: That's tough, just too, too bad. Something like me is the best they're going to get, and that's if they get anything at all. But as I said, I'm not positive about any of this, so let's forget the God blather for now. If I had a head, I'd have a headache. What do you say?

ME: Okay, thy will be done, if you say so. Let's just listen to some music, assuming you have ears on your nonexistent head.

GOD: Yeah. (God laughs.)

ME: Yeah. (I wake up.)

The Universality Argument
(and the Relevance of Morality and Mathematics)

C. S. Lewis wrote, "If anyone will take the trouble to compare the moral teaching of, say, the ancient Egyptians, Babylonians, Hindus, Chinese, Greeks and Romans, what will really strike him will be how very like they are to each other and to our own." He concluded that the moral sense, what Immanuel Kant called "the Moral Law," our intuitive feeling for right and wrong, is universal and instilled in us by God.

Schematically, the argument from the universality of moral values is the following:

1. Across cultures the similarities in what's considered right or wrong are strikingly apparent.

2. The best explanation for these similarities is that they stem from God.
3. Therefore God exists.

Kant's version of the argument is a little more subtle, but also assumes that moral standards are real, objective, and universal.

Of course, proponents of the argument don't say much about the blasphemers, disobedient sons, homosexuals, Sabbath workers, and others who, the Bible demands, should be stoned to death. Happily, even most believers today don't believe this. Nor do they expatiate on the similarities of the draconian constraints on women—single, married, or widowed—sanctioned by Christian, Muslim, and Hindu theology. The general point is that, contrary to Assumption 1, the similarity of moral codes across cultures is either somewhat dubious except on the broadest level—murder, theft, child care, basic honesty—or else not something proponents wish to herald.

Assumption 2 is even weaker than Assumption 1. There is a compelling and irreligious alternative to it: an evolutionary explanation for the similarity of moral codes. Humans, even before they were humans, have always had to deal with a set of basic requirements. How will they get food, keep warm, protect themselves from predators and other humans, mate, and reproduce? Any group that doesn't meet these basic requirements doesn't last long.

Moreover, these requirements are quite constraining and lead, more or less, to the prohibition of unprovoked murder and theft, to an insistence on basic honesty, a concern for children, and so on. The details are no doubt interesting and intricate and have been the subject of several recent books, in particular *Moral Minds* by the biologist Marc D. Hauser. Their rough conclusion, however, is that groups that allowed infractions of these broad codes of conduct would be less likely to thrive and reproduce; murdering one's neighbors and killing one's own children are not activities that conduce to the success of any group. These natural constraints, rather than commandments from a God, are the reason for whatever rough similarity of moral codes there is across cultures.

Another counterargument to the argument from morality deserves mention. Similar to the argument on the source of natural law, it derives from the question of why God chose the particular moral laws that He did (or, as Judeo-Christian tradition has it, that He inscribed on stone tablets). If He chose the laws capriciously, then it makes little sense to say that God is good, since He arbitrarily concocted the very notion of the good Himself. On the other hand, if God chose the laws He did because they are the correct ones and encapsulate the good, then their correctness and the good are independent notions that don't require God. Furthermore, He is presumably Himself subject to the preexisting moral laws, in which case there's once again little reason to introduce Him as an intermediary between the moral laws and humans.

God's goodness is also the issue in the classic problem of evil dating back to the Greek atheist Epicurus. "God either wishes to take away evil and is unable, or He is able and unwilling, or He is neither willing nor able, or He is both willing and able." In the first three cases He is not very God-like; either He's feeble, malevolent, or both. Only in the fourth case is He suitably God-like, which prompts you to wonder about the prevalence and persistence of evil. Or, to make the situation more concrete, imagine a serial child killer with his thirtieth victim tied before him. Prayers for the child are offered by many. If God is either unable or unwilling to stop the killer, what good is He? It seems that the usual response to this is that we don't understand His ways, but if this is true, once again you must ask why introduce Him in the first place? Is there such a shortage of things we don't understand that we need to manufacture another?

Of course, it's not hard to find inconsistencies in even the most basic religious doctrines and beliefs. According to Christians, for example, God sacrificed His Son, Jesus, in order that we might live forever. But does an omnipotent being really need to sacrifice? Are His resources limited? And if God did this for us, why was He not more transparent in His actions and offerings rather than demanding that we blindly subscribe to statements written in an opaque, contradictory book? If He loved us so much, why would unending torment be the consequence of choosing skepticism over faith? Why would God state, in effect, that if you don't believe in Him, then too bad for you (hell, that is)? And on and on.

I almost feel silly making these observations. They may strike some as childish, but characterizing them as child-like would be more accurate. It seems to me that any child unencumbered by imposed dogma would ask such obvious questions and note such obvious inconsistencies.

These inconsistencies, like the one between omniscience and omnipotence, bring to mind a larger logical issue of relevance to theological (and other) speculations: the so-called Boolean satisfiability problem. Despite its ungainly name, the problem poses a natural question. Say you're committed to a collection of complicated statements about your beliefs, the world, and God. Is there a quick way to determine whether this collection, made up of simple propositions and tied together with the logical connectives "and," "or," and "not," really is satisfiable? That is, how do we determine if there is any way of assigning truth or falsity to the simple propositions that will result in all of the complicated statements in the collection being simultaneously true?

There are websites that illustrate this problem for theological assertions. They ask visitors to say whether complicated statements about their beliefs, the world, and God are true or false. Then, after they've done so, the site more often than not informs the visitors that their assertions have resulted in an inconsistency. More generally, it turns out that there probably is no quick way (technically, a way in "polynomial time") to determine the consistency of large collections of statements. If there were, a whole bunch of other mathematical and logical problems would be more quickly solved than they're assumed to be. (The satisfiability problem, an important one in theoretical computer science, is what logicians call NP-complete, NP being short for "nondeterministic polynomial time.")

Staying with logical and mathematical matters, I note that a resolution similar to that for the argument from the universality of moral values works as well for a comparable argument based on the universality and applicability of logic and mathematics.

Mathematicians have long been interested in applications of mathematics and long noted its universality. Throughout the world, for example, pi, the ratio of the circumference of a circle to its diameter, is the same number, approximately 3.14 (except in the Bible, where inerrancy apparently extends to only one significant figure and it's stated to be 3). And whether in physics, chemistry, or economics and whether in Brazil, India, or Italy, mathematics solves a disparate array of problems, ranging from the mundane aspects of bookkeeping to the ethereal realms of astronomy.

Both mathematicians and physicists have been particularly fascinated with the latter. Archimedes' concern with grains of sand that would fit into the universe; with moving the earth with a very long lever; with minuscule units of time and other quantities whose repeated sums necessarily exceed any magnitude—all these speak of the early origin of the association between number fascination and a concern with time and space. Blaise Pascal wondered about faith, calculation, and man's place in nature, which is, as he put it, midway between the infinite and the nothing. Nietzsche speculated about a closed and infinitely recurring universe. Henri Poincaré and others with an intuitionist or constructivist approach to mathematics have compared the sequence of whole numbers to our pre-theoretic conception of time as a sequence of discrete instants. Georg Cantor's set theory and the analysis of Augustin Cauchy, among many others, resolved many paradoxes of infinity but led to still others. Riemann, Gauss, Einstein, Gödel, and countless others have made conjectures about space, time, and infinity that, as even this short list demonstrates, have long been a staple of mathematico-physical-spiritual reflections.

The applicability and universality of mathematics aren't often taken as an argument for the existence of God, however. If they were, the argument might run something like the following:

1. Mathematics seems ideally suited to describing the physical world.

2. This uncanny suitability is no accident.
3. It is evidence of a greater harmony and universality ultimately attributable to a creator.
4. Therefore this creator, God, exists.

As noted, these ideas have a distinguished mathematical pedigree, but not until the physicist Eugene Wigner's famous 1960 paper "The Unreasonable Effectiveness of Mathematics in the Natural Sciences" were they made quite explicit. In it Wigner maintained that the ability of mathematics to describe and predict the physical world is no accident but rather evidence of deep and mysterious harmony. He further argued that "the enormous usefulness of mathematics in the natural sciences is something bordering on the mysterious and . . . there is no rational explanation for it."

But is the usefulness of mathematics, although indubitable, really so mysterious? It seems to me that as with the argument from moral universality there is a quite compelling alternative explanation. Why is mathematics so useful? Well, we count, we measure, we employ basic logic, and these activities were stimulated by ubiquitous aspects of the physical world. Even such common experiences as standing up straight, pushing and pulling objects, and moving about in the world prepare us to form quasi-mathematical ideas and to internalize the associations among them.

The size of a collection (of stones, grapes, animals), for

example, is associated with the size of a number, and keeping track of its size leads to counting. Putting collections together is associated with adding numbers, and so on. The only presupposition necessary for these basic arithmetic operations is that objects maintain their identity; you can't put together different collections of water drops. Contrary to a famous remark by the mathematician Leopold Kronecker, who wrote, "God made the integers, all the rest is the work of man," even the whole numbers were the work of man.

Another animating metaphor associates the familiar realm of measuring sticks (small branches, say, or pieces of string) with the more abstract one of geometry. The length of a stick is associated with the size of a number once some specified segment is associated with the number 1, and relations between the numbers associated with a triangle, say, are noted. Scores and scores of such metaphors underlying other, more advanced mathematical disciplines have been developed by the linguist George Lakoff and the psychologist Rafael Núñez in their intriguing book *Where Mathematics Comes From*.

Once part of human practice, these notions are abstracted, idealized, and formalized to create basic mathematics. The deductive nature of mathematics then makes this formalization useful in realms to which it is only indirectly related. We use logic to progress from the patently obvious axioms suggested to us by everyday practices to much less manifest propositions on to sometimes quite counterintuitive theorems and factoids, say about the Fibonacci sequence. (Since it seems that every popular book that touches on religion must include the obligatory mention of the Fibonacci sequence, I shall not let its complete irrelevance here prevent me from irrelevantly mentioning it as well.)

Simple properties of multiplication lead soon enough to combinatorial identities that seem almost incredible in their ability to connect quite disparate phenomena. Obvious facts of everyday geometry give rise to astonishing insights into the nature of space. We construct the real numbers, say, the irrational square root of 2, out of more prosaic whole numbers (technically out of equivalence classes of Cauchy sequences or Dedekind cuts of rational numbers). In a difficult-to-define sense, all of these mathematical objects, although growing out of our quotidian experiences, exist independently of us, only seemingly in some Platonic realm beyond time or space.

The universe acts on us, we adapt to it, and the notions that we develop as a result, including the mathematical ones, are in a sense taught us by the universe. Evolution has selected those of our ancestors (both human and not) whose behavior and thought were consistent with the workings of the universe. The aforementioned French mathematician Henri Poincaré, who came within a hairbreadth of discovering special relativity, agreed. He wrote,

"By natural selection our mind has adapted itself to the conditions of the external world. It has adopted the geometry most advantageous to the species or, in other words, the most convenient." The usefulness of mathematics, it seems, is not so unreasonable.

Many have written of the abstract principles and utility of morality in a way reminiscent of Bertrand Russell's comment about the "cold, austere beauty" of mathematics. The evolutionary sources of morality and mathematics remind us of the warm bodies from which this beauty and usefulness arise.

The Gambling Argument
(and Emotions from Prudence to Fear)

Dread and hope, prudence and calculation: these are the ingredients of the argument from fear and the more mathematical argument from gambling. The latter argument possesses many variants, the most well-known of which dates back to the famous wager proposed by the seventeenth-century French philosopher Blaise Pascal:

1. We can choose to believe God exists, or we can choose not to so believe.
2. If we reject God and act accordingly, we risk everlasting agony and torment if He does exist (what statisticians call a Type I error) but enjoy fleeting earthly delights if He doesn't.

3. If we accept God and act accordingly, we risk little if He doesn't exist (what's called a Type II error) but enjoy endless heavenly bliss if He does.

4. It's in our self-interest to accept God's existence.

5. Therefore God exists.

Pascal's wager, originally stated in Christian terms, was an argument for becoming a Christian. Only if one already believes in Christian doctrine, however, as Pascal did, does this argument have any persuasive power. The argument itself has little to do with Christianity and could just as readily be used by practitioners of Islam and other religions to rationalize other already existing beliefs.

Sometimes Pascal's argument for believing in God is phrased in terms of the mathematical notion of an expected value. The average or expected value of a quantity is the sum of the products of the values it might assume multiplied by these values' respective probabilities. So, for example, imagine an especially munificent lottery. It gives you a 99 percent chance of winning $100 and a 1 percent chance of winning $50,000. In this case, the expected value of your winnings would be (.99 × $100) + (.01 × $50,000), which sums to $599. That is, if you played this lottery over and over again, the average value of your winnings per play would be $599.

In the case of Pascal's wager we can perform similar calculations to determine the expected values of the two choices (to believe or not to believe). Each of these expected values depends on the probability of God's existence and the payoffs associated with the two possibilities: yes, He does, or no, He doesn't. If we multiply whatever huge numerical payoff we put on endless heavenly bliss by even a tiny probability, we obtain a product that trumps all other factors, and gambling prudence dictates that we should believe (or at least try hard to do so).

Another problem associated with assigning such disproportionate payoffs to God's existence and the eternal happiness to be derived from obeying Him is that this assignment itself can serve to rationalize the most hateful of actions. Contrary to Dostoyevsky's warning that "if God doesn't exist, everything is allowed," we have the fanatical believer's threat that "if God does exist, everything is allowed." Killing thousands or even millions of people might be justified in some devout believers' eyes if in doing so they violate only mundane human laws and incur only mundane human penalties while upholding higher divine laws and earning higher divine approbation.

I should note parenthetically that attaching a probability to God's existence in the above argument or for other purposes such as ascribing attributes to Him is a futile and wrongheaded undertaking. Even the phrase "the probability of God's existence," like much religious talk and writing, seems to be infected with "category errors" and other "linguistic diseases," therapy for which has long occupied analytic philosophers going back to Ludwig Wittgenstein, Gilbert Ryle, and J. L. Austin.

But forget probability for the moment. Is it even clear what "God is" statements mean? Echoing Bill Clinton, I note that they depend on what the meaning of "is" is. Here, for example, are three possible meanings of "is" involving God: (1) God is complexity; (2) God is omniscient; (3) there is a God. The first "is" is the "is" of identity; it's symbolized by $G = C$. The second "is" is the "is" of predication; G has the property omniscience, symbolized by $O(G)$. The third "is" is existential; there is, or there exists, an entity that is God-like, symbolized by $\exists xG(x)$. (It's not hard to equivocally move back and forth between these meanings of "is" to arrive at quite dubious conclusions. For example, from "God is love," "Love is blind," and "My father's brother is blind," we might conclude, "There is a God, and he is my uncle.")

Of course, we shouldn't get too literal. Many seeming references to God are naturally rephrased without the references. "God only knows" often means "No one really knows," for example, and "God willing" sometimes means nothing more than "If things work out okay." More generally, phrases that have the same grammar in a natural language needn't share the same presuppositions and logic. Consider "going on to infinity" versus "going on to New York," "honesty compels me" versus "the Mafia compels me," "before the world began" versus "before the war began," and "the probability of a royal flush" versus "the probability of a God."

With regard to the last opposition, "the probability of a royal flush" makes sense because we can calculate how many poker hands and royal flushes are possible, determine that all hands are equally likely, and so on. But returning to "the probability of a God," I note that it fails to make sense, in part because the universe is unique. Or if some physical theories suggest otherwise, we have no way of knowing how many universes there are, whether they're equally likely, how many have a God, and so on. And clearly the latter questions border on the nonsensical no matter how nebulous our notion of probability. Unfortunately, none of this prevented the mathematician and physicist Stephen Unwin from attempting to assign numerical values to these questions in his book *The Probability of God*.

In any case, despite its mathematical overlay, Pascal's wager possesses an appeal not much different from that of the powerful old argument from fear—fear of missing out on heavenly bliss, fear of suffering unending torment, fear of dying:

1. If God doesn't exist, we and our loved ones are going to die.
2. This is sad, dreadful, frightening.
3. Therefore God exists.

Again, it's easy to understand the initial attraction of this argument. Anyone who has lost someone close longs for his or her return. Sadly and oh so obviously, this doesn't happen. After my father died, I better understood the divine placebo and the profound difference between the religious outlook of "Our Father which art in heaven" and the irreligious one of "my father, who art nowhere." Still, we think with our heads, and the argument is clearly bogus and even offensive.

A different reason for the appeal of the argument from fear is the common psycho-political tendency of people to rally around a political leader in dangerous times. People seek protection when they feel threatened. This is, of course, why leaders often resort to fearmongering to attain or remain in power. And who but God might be the greatest "leader" of all?

Not surprisingly, this dynamic is a common one in political contexts as well. A recent illustration is Ron Suskind's book *The One Percent Doctrine*. In it he writes that Vice President Dick Cheney forcefully maintained that the war on terror empowered the Bush administration to act without the need for evidence. Suskind describes the Cheney doctrine as follows: "Even if there's just a 1 percent chance of the unimaginable coming due, act as if it is a certainty." This simplistic doctrine of "If at least 1 percent, then act" is especially frightening in international conflicts, not least because the number of threats misconstrued (by someone or other) to meet the 1 percent threshold is huge and the consequences of military action are so terrible and irrevocable. Like Pascal's wager, the extremely negative consequences of disbelief are taken to be sufficient to overcome their small probability and ensure that the expected value of action exceeds that of inaction.

The connections among morality, prudence, and religion are complicated and beyond my concerns here. I would like to counter, however, the claim regularly made by religious people that atheists and agnostics are somehow less moral or law-abiding than they. There is absolutely no evidence for this, and I suspect whatever average difference there is along the nebulous dimension of morality has the opposite algebraic sign.

Pascal's wager notwithstanding, studies on crime rates (and other measures of social dysfunction) showing that nonbelievers in the United States are extremely underrepresented in prison suggest as much. So does Japan, one of the world's least crime-ridden countries, only a minority of whose citizens reportedly believe in God. And so, too, do those aforementioned monomaniacal true believers whose smiling surety often harbors a toxic intolerance. (Recall the physicist Steven Weinberg's happy quip "With or without religion, good people will do good, and evil people will do evil, but for good people to do evil, that takes religion.") Also worthy of mention are the garden-variety religious scoundrels, hypocrites, and charlatans in public life. Not quite evil, but also far from admirable, is the social opportunism that no doubt is the reason for many expressions of religious humbug. Like feigning an interest in golf to get ahead in business, mouthing the right pieties can often improve one's prospects in politics.

An atheist or agnostic who acts morally simply because it is the right thing to do is, in a sense, more moral than someone who is trying to avoid everlasting torment or, as is the case with martyrs, to achieve eternal bliss. He or she is making the moral choice without benefit of Pascal's divine bribe. This choice is all the more impressive when an atheist or agnostic sacrifices his or her life, for example, to rescue a drowning child, aware that there'll be no heavenly reward for this lifesaving valor. The contrast with acts motivated by calculated expected value or uncalculated unexpected fear (or, worse, fearlessness) is stark.

Still, people do often vigorously insist that religious beliefs are necessary to ensure moral behavior. Though the claim is quite clearly false of people in general, there is a sense in which it might be true if one has been brought up in a very religious environment. A classic experiment on the so-called overjustification effect by the psychologists David Greene, Betty Sternberg, and Mark Lepper is relevant. They exposed fourth- and fifth-grade students to a variety of intriguing mathematical games and measured the time the children played them. They found that the children seemed to possess a good deal of intrinsic interest in the games. The games were fun. After a few days, however, the psychologists began to reward the children for playing; those playing them more had a better chance of winning the prizes offered. The prizes did increase the time the children played the games, but when the prizes were stopped, the children lost almost all interest in the games and rarely played them. The extrinsic rewards had undercut the children's intrinsic interest. Likewise, religious injunctions and rewards promised to children for being good might, if repudiated in later life, drastically reduce the time people spend playing the "being good" game. This is another reason not to base ethics on religious teachings.

In conclusion, emotional arguments from fear, hope, and fervency are very easy to refute but especially difficult to successfully oppose since, despite their occasional mathematical garb, their appeal circumvents, subverts, bypasses, and undermines the critical faculties of many. Moreover, since literal truth is not always the paramount concern of people, it seems that the untruths underlying faith may make ordinary life more bearable.

Atheists, Agnostics, and "Brights"

Given the starkly feeble arguments for God's existence, one might suspect—that is, if one lived on a different planet—that atheism would be well accepted, perhaps even approved of. Living on this planet and specifically in the United States, with its public figures' increasingly common references to God and faith, one shouldn't be too surprised that this isn't so. Bearing this out, a recent study (one among many others that have come to similar conclusions) finds that Americans are not fond of atheists and trust them less than they do other groups.

The depth of this distrust is a bit astonishing, not to mention disturbing and depressing. More than two thousand randomly selected people were interviewed by researchers from the University of Minnesota in 2006. Asked whether they would disapprove of a child's wish to marry an athe-ist, 47.6 percent of those interviewed said yes. Asked the same question about Muslims and African-Americans, the yes responses fell to 33.5 percent and 27.2 percent, respec-tively. The yes responses for Asian-Americans, Hispan-ics, Jews, and conservative Christians were 18.5 percent, 18.5 percent, 11.8 percent, and 6.9 percent, respectively. The margin of error was a bit over 2 percent.

When asked which groups did not share their vision of American society, 39.5 percent of those interviewed men-tioned atheists. Asked the same question about Muslims and homosexuals, the figures dropped to a slightly less de-pressing 26.3 percent and 22.6 percent, respectively. For Hispanics, Jews, Asian-Americans, and African-Americans, they fell further to 7.6 percent, 7.4 percent, 7.0 percent, and 4.6 percent, respectively.

The study contains other results, but these are suffi-cient to underline its gist: atheists are seen by many Amer-icans (especially conservative Christians) as alien and are, in the words of the sociologist Penny Edgell, the study's lead researcher, "a glaring exception to the rule of increas-ing tolerance over the last 30 years."

Edgell also maintains that atheists seem to be outside the limits of American morality, which has largely been defined by religion. Many of those interviewed saw athe-ists as cultural elitists or amoral materialists or given to criminal behavior or drugs. The study states, "Our find-ings seem to rest on a view of atheists as self-interested individuals who are not concerned with the common good." Of course, I repeat—I hope unnecessarily—that belief in God isn't at all necessary to have a keen ethical concern for others, the smug certainty of the benighted notwithstanding. An odd example of this benightedness is the fact that the state of Arkansas has not yet roused itself to rescind Article 19 (no doubt unenforced) of its constitution: "No person who denies the being of a God shall hold any office in the civil departments of this State, nor be competent to testify as a witness in any court." Half a dozen other states have similar laws.

The above and similar studies, as well as many other instances of such witless attitudes, suggest a couple of very partial remedies, one a bit droll, the other quite earnest. The first is a movie analogy of *Brokeback Mountain*, the film that dealt with manly cowboys coming to grips with their homosexuality. A dramatic rendition of a devoutly religious person (or couple) coming to grips with the slowly dawning realization of his (their) disbelief may be eye-opening for many. A movie version of the science writer Martin Gardner's novel *The Flight of Peter Fromm* may do the trick. In the book Gardner tells the story of a young fundamentalist and his somewhat torturous journey to freethinking skepticism. An irreligious television series or soap opera with the same focus may help as well. (Supply your proposed title here.)

The second, more substantial response to the bias against atheists and agnostics has been a proposal to refer to them by another name. But what do you call someone who is not religious? And is there really a need for a new name for such people? The philosopher Daniel Dennett and a number of others believe so. They have pushed for the adoption of a new term to signify someone who holds a naturalistic (as opposed to a religious) worldview. Dennett defended the need for such a term by noting that a 2002 survey by the Pew Forum on Religion and Public Life found that approximately twenty-five million Americans are atheists or agnostics or (the largest category) have no religious preference.

The statistic is not definitive, of course. Polls like this one and the study cited above are crude instruments for clarifying the varieties of human belief and disbelief. Moreover, since the polls rely on the self-reporting of sometimes unpopular opinions, the number of nonbelievers may be much higher.

In any case, the problematic new term that has been proposed for nonreligious people who value evidence and eschew obfuscation is "Bright" (usually capitalized), and the coinage is by Paul Geisert and Mynga Futrell. They have started an Internet group, the Brights, intended to further the influence of Brights. On their website they state: "Currently the naturalistic worldview is insufficiently expressed within most cultures. The purpose of this movement is to form an umbrella Internet constituency of individuals having social and political recognition and power. There is a great diversity of persons who have a naturalistic worldview. Under this broad umbrella, as Brights, these people can gain social and political influence in a society infused with supernaturalism."

I don't much like the term, preferring the, to me, more honest alternatives "atheist," "agnostic," or even "infidel." Furthermore, I don't think a degree in public relations is needed to expect that many people will construe "Bright" as pretentious or worse. To defuse such criticism, defenders of the term stress that "Bright" should not be confused with "bright." Just as "gay" now has an additional new meaning, quite distinct from its old one, so, it's argued, will "Bright." It should be noted, of course, that there are in this country not only millions of Brights but millions of religious people who are bright, just as there are many in both categories who are not so bright.

Putting the problems with the term "Bright" aside, however, I believe the attempt to recognize this large group of Americans is a most welcome development. One reason is that there are many Brights, and it's always healthy to recognize facts. Another is that, as Darwin said about evolution, "there is a grandeur in this (naturalistic) view of life." Yet another reason is that these people, whatever their appellation, have interests that some sort of organization might help further.

The diffidence of unbelievers and their reluctance to announce themselves may be one factor, for example, in the distressingly robust flirtation between church and state here in the United States. From its many faith-based initiatives to its swaggering conflation of religious and secular matters, the Bush administration has been particularly unsympathetic to Brights. (Quite apt here, as well as at a number of other places in this book, is the line from William Butler Yeats: "The best lack all conviction, while the worst are full of passionate intensity." Less eloquent, but more personal, is one of my father's favorite words, "piffle," which he used whenever he heard blowhards expounding some bit of malarkey. Polite guy that he was, he usually just whispered his piffles to his family.)

The issue is nonpartisan. There is certainly no shortage of Brights in any political party. Given that Brights are far from rare, it is reasonable to ask future candidates for president or other political office to state their attitude toward them (designated by whatever term they choose). We might also speculate about which candidates might be closet Brights. Forget atheism or agnosticism. Who among them would even evince anything like the freethinking of theists such as Thomas Jefferson and Abraham Lincoln? Who would put forward a Bright Supreme Court nominee? Who would support self-avowed Brights in positions of authority over children? Who would even include Brights in inclusive platitudes about Catholics, Protestants, Jews, and Muslims? Doing so might be good politics. Although unorganized and relatively invisible, the irreligious constitute a large group to whom politicians almost never appeal.

Moreover, it would be interesting to see and hear the squirming responses of the candidates to the above questions.

Back to the term "Bright." Richard Dawkins, who coined the useful term "meme" (which refers to any idea, habit, word, song lyric, fashion, and such that passes from one person to another by a sort of viral mimicry), is particularly interested in how contagious this particular meme will be. An advocate of the term "Bright," he wonders whether it will proliferate as quickly as backward baseball caps, exposed navels, "fun" as an adjective, and locutions like "Duh," or simply wither away. Will the Internet be a factor? Will the term appear cool or smack of silly trendiness?

Whether called freethinkers, nonbelievers, skeptics, atheists, agnostics, secular humanists, God-deniers, the irreligious, Yeah-ists, or whatever, Brights have been around in large numbers since at least the Enlightenment (the Enbrightenment?). So even if this particular term for them fades (and despite employing it herein, I hope it does), what won't disappear is their determination to quietly think for themselves and not be cowed by the ignorant and overbearing religiosity of so many earnestly humorless people.

To end on a note implicit throughout this book, I think the world would benefit if more people of diverse backgrounds were to admit to being irreligious. Perhaps a more realistic hope is for more to acknowledge at least their own private doubts about God. While not a panacea, candidly recognizing the absence of any good logical arguments for God's existence, giving up on divine allies and advocates as well as taskmasters and tormentors, and prizing a humane, reasonable, and brave outlook just might help move this world a bit closer to a heaven on earth.

And whether we're Bright, schmight, religious, or irreligious, I think that's what 96.39 percent of us want.

INDEX

Printed in the USA
CPSIA information can be obtained
at www.ICGtesting.com
LVHW091145150724
785511LV00005B/543

9 780809 059188